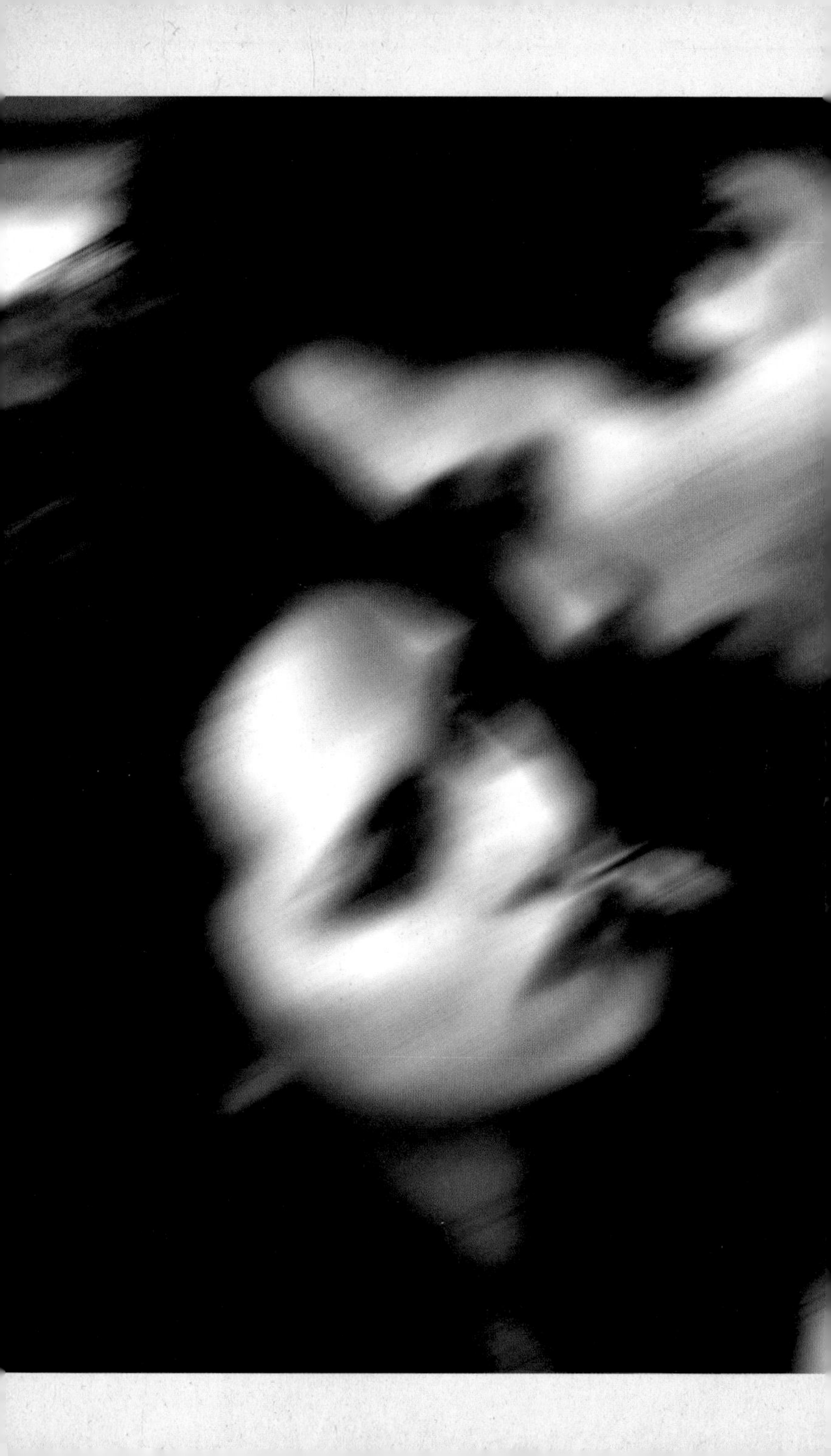

THE STORY OF HOW WE MADE THE MOVIE

based on the novel by STEPHENIE MEYER

CATHERINE HARDWICKE

LITTLE, BROWN AND COMPANY
New York Boston

COVER CREDITS:
ART © DEANA NEWCOMB: Front Photos: Row 1, lt; Row 2 rt, far rt; Row 3 rt; Row 4 lt; Row 5 lt; Row 7 rt; Back Photos: Row 2 rt; Row 6 rt; Row 7 two mid, rt; Row 8 rt. photo. ART © KATHY SHORKEY: Front Illustration: Row 1 mid, Back Illustration: Row 7, lt. ART © TREVOR GORING: Front Storyboard: Row 1 rt. Back: Row 1 lt. ART © PETER SOREL: Front Photos: Row 2 lt, Row 7 far rt, Back: Row 1 rt, Row 4 mid lt, Row 5 lt, Row 7 far lt. ART © JAMES LIN: Back Photo: Row 4, lt. ART © PATRICK LOUNGWAY: Front Frame Grab: Row 3 lt. ART © IRENE HARDWICKE OLIVIERI: Front Painting: Row 4 and 5 rt. ART © BEN HARDWICKE: Front Photo: Row 7 lt, Back: Row 6 rt. ART © PATRICK T. SMITH: Back Photo: Row 4 far lt. ART © SUMMIT ENTERTAINMENT: Front Promo Photos: Row 3 mid, Row 6 rt, Row 8 lt, Back: Row 6 lt. Row 8 lt. Spine: top & bottom. ART © PHIL KELLER: Front Storyboards: row 6 lt. mid. Back: row 3 all. ART © CATHERINE HARDWICKE: All hand lettering, Front Photos: Row 7 mid, Back: Row 2 lt, Row 4 mid rt, Row 8 lt. ART © OKSANA NEDAVNIAYA: Front Illustrations: Row 8 mid, Back: Row 4/5 far rt, Row 5 far lt

Little, Brown and Company

Hachette Book Group
237 Park Avenue, New York, NY 10017
Visit our Web site at www.lb-teens.com

Little, Brown and Company is a division of Hachette Book Group, Inc. The Little, Brown name and logo are trademarks of Hachette Book Group, Inc.

Library of Congress Control Number: 2009922106
ISBN 978-0-316-07052-2
First Edition: March 2009
10 9 8 7 6 5 4 3
WOR
Printed in the United States of America

for the fabulous Stephenie, who started it all...
and my sister Irene, whose mysterious paintings
inspire me daily ... and for my mother
Jamee who insisted several times that
I cast a "hot" Edward.

table of contents

THE NEW YORK TIMES BESTSELLER

twilight

STEPHENIE MEY

Making Twilight

In January of 2007, I bought a copy of "Twilight"— and devoured it. This is a photo of how my book looks now: dozens of Post-Its, underlined passages, hundreds of hi-lited favorite lines with notes in the margin like "this has to be in the movie!" My challenge was to translate this to film. How to take Stephenie's powerful emotions— delirious, obsessive, hypnotic, profound love and put that on screen. Make you feel what she makes you feel when you read her words – when you let yourself get swept away with Bella and Edward ... when you imagine the Cullens – a vegetarian vampire clan living secretly in the Pacific Rainforest... full of ancient treetrunks covered in moss and ground covered in ferns. And fog – always deep, thick mysterious fog. In this book, I try to show fans and aspiring filmmakers the process that my crew and I went through while making Twilight.

Catherine

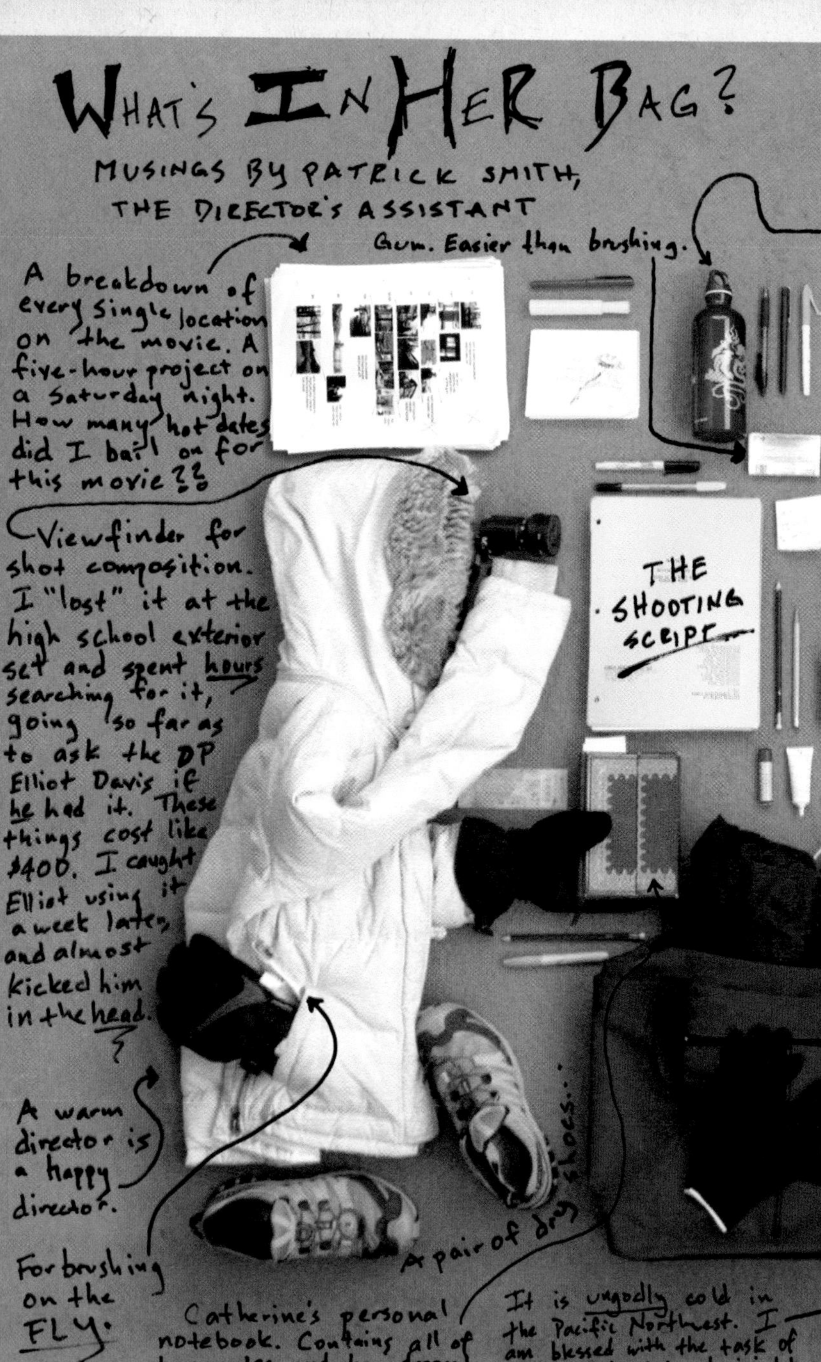
WHAT'S IN HER BAG?
MUSINGS BY PATRICK SMITH, THE DIRECTOR'S ASSISTANT
A breakdown of every single location on the movie. A five-hour project on a Saturday night. How many hot dates did I bail on for this movie??
Gum. Easier than brushing.
Viewfinder for shot composition. I "lost" it at the high school exterior set and spent hours searching for it, going so far as to ask the DP Elliot Davis if he had it. These things cost like $400. I caught Elliot using it a week later, and almost kicked him in the head.
THE SHOOTING SCRIPT
A warm director is a happy director.
For brushing on the FLY.
A pair of dry shoes...
Catherine's personal notebook. Contains all of her notes and her deepest, innermost thoughts. If I lose it, I get my head cut off and put out as a warning to other assistants.
It is ungodly cold in the Pacific Northwest. I am blessed with the task of handing off a hat and rain jacket if it's about to pour, gloves if it's too windy, and fresh socks. Wearing fresh socks at midday feels... DELICIOUS.

Can someone please explain to me why I bought an overpriced water bottle for CH, and there are STILL empty plastic bottles all over my car?
SHOTLISTS!! Why sleep when you can make them ALL NIGHT LONG??
All of Cat's pens are CHEWED UP!
Look out, ladies! It's Solomon Trimble!
OUR BIBLE
Cat's ID card from McAllen High School. That's how prepared she is... never know if you might need it.
In an act of temporary insanity Cat got laser beams shot into her eyes (LASIK Surgery). Gotta keep those peepers moist.
Catherine uses her iphone to work. I use mine to watch videos of TALKING CATS.
On any given scout, you will find this on her hip.
Cat puts stickers all over her computer to dissuade thieves.
CH's backpack. Total estimated weight: 40 pounds. Leaves her side: never. Guess who gets to carry it?
Contains all manner of documents. Shotlists, script, budget, reference photos, notes, director's plans... everything you need to direct TWILIGHT.
She plugs this into the car's cigarette lighter to power her electronic devices. DON'T LEAVE HOME WITHOUT IT!

this made me think of the meadow...
detail of a PAINTING by my sister Irene Hardwicke Olivieri

"Warmth, moisture, light."

MY INSPIRATION

My sister paints these dreamy layered images of men and women in nature - often with very personal handwriting on every surface.

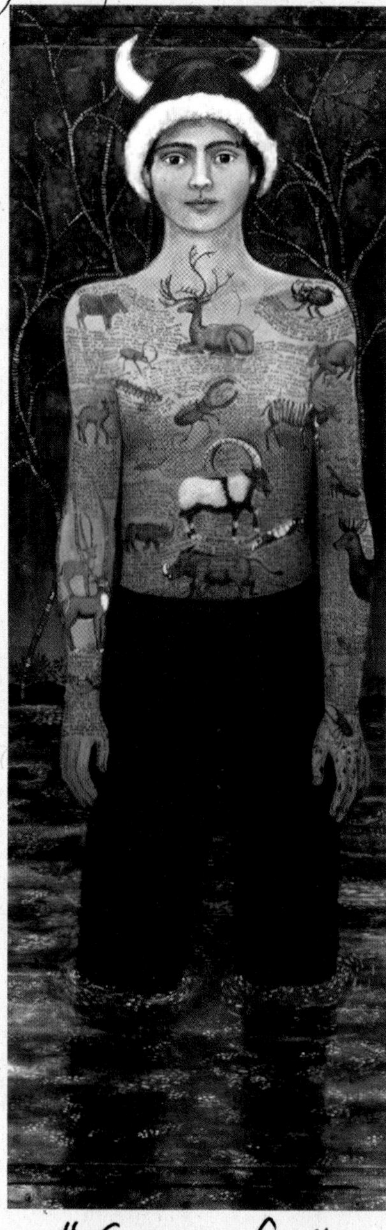

The paintings feel intimate, almost like a diary,
almost like .... Twilight....

"Coarse fur"

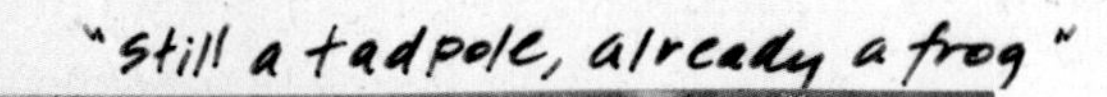

"still a tadpole, already a frog"

thinking of Bella....

"Quicksand"

Erin Schneider took these evocative shots of Sarah Blakley-Cartwright, my "adopted" daughter. They have the "Bella feel"—loose hair, natural make-up, and a connection to the outdoors.

TRIVIA ALERT: find Sarah in about a dozen Twilight scenes. She is the only actor in all 4 of my films.

BELLA
I thought maybe Edward could show off his skills by spelling out Bella's name in logs.
Some of my first sketches
EXTREME CLOSE-UPS TO DRAW YOU INTO BELLA'S EMOTIONS — ABSTRACT-SUBJECTIVE CAMERAWORK
THE ESSENCE OF THE FILM - TENSION LEADING UP TO FIRST KISS.
Kristen has that magic luminescent skin that glows.
CONFESSION: I LOVE MOSS.
Wah!
Magnificent old growth trees- connection to Nature
How did Bambi get up in that tree?

TRIVIA NOTE:

I wore this "SAINTS" BRACELET every shoot day and so did Bella. (except in 3 scenes). cost: $2.00 venice boardwalk.

one of my favorite fotos from the first location scout in Forks — green trees disappearing into the mist . . .

Location Scouting

I shot this trippy photo out the window of the plane on our first location scout. Sept, 2007.

Jamie Marshall, ↑ co-producer and 1st A.D., poses for James ON A LOCATION scout at the "Shire" in Washington.

I usually act out the scenes when we location scout – Here I thought that Bella + Jacob could balance on the big driftwood logs at La Push Beach.

For the scene where the Nomads kill Waylon, I wanted a dramatic new location. We scouted "Kato's Marina" and I took this eerie "STALKER" shot. ↙

On New Year's Day, 2008, I was location scouting with Beth Melnick when I suddenly saw the "GOD RAYS!" We pulled over and I shot this photo which became the inspiration for the light in the Meadow.

"The Look" of Twilight

Elliot shot this photo at La Push Beach. It demonstrates our color palette — cool blues, dark rich blacks, grays, back lit mist.

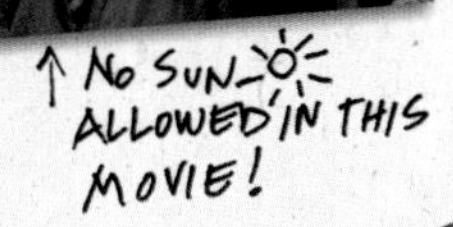

↑ No SUN ☼ ALLOWED IN THIS MOVIE!

Elliot studies the "new" meadow location — with its deep greens — it's beautiful but very difficult to work there — slippery rocks & no level places to put lights or dolly tracks.

CLOUD COVER = BEAUTIFUL SOFT LIGHT = FREQUENT RAIN

THE CAMERA HAS TO BE PROTECTED.

Cinematography & Color Palette

Throw broken ~~glass~~ mirrors —
like Ninja stars....

Subjective — through the rays

silhouettes flying through
glass
falling
rain...
diamonds

Bodies are hurling at her
and coming at her

In the book —
she thinks she died
she think she died.

Dark forms — out of focus —
flying through the light...
Point source — shafts of light...
Blurry out of focus —
Forms — — —

Hallation...
Near death experience state.
Bodies float in front of her...

GLASS RAINS DOWN
~~over~~ over...

V.O. I died...

window
glass
crystal....

Elliot Davis — cinematographer or Director of Photography or D.P. has worked with me on all four of my films. His eye is legendary — as is his amazing ability to shoot hand-held, subjective shots. These are pages from our first meeting where we brainstormed about how the ballet studio could look.

Here's Elliot "pre-lighting" the ballet studio set — Setting up the beams. ↙

I called Melissa Rosenberg, the screenwriter, and told her: "Guess what – they surf at La Push. Awesome, huh? So we added surfing into the scenes.

Volume 77, No. 31

inside:

Year in Review
• Top 2007 news, sports
at a glance.
See page 13.

Insight Schools ins
• Online school de
wows QVSD board.
See page 21.

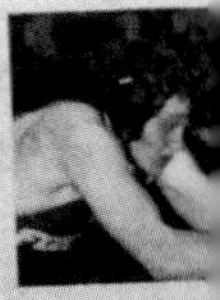

Wrestlers win lea
• Spartan wrestlers
Southwest Washing
See page 25.

After returning from a scout – I showed this photo to Elliot and we realized this was a great model for the meadow sequence. Edward could step out from behind a dark silhouette of a tree to reveal himself in the sunlight.

KS FORUM

PRSRT STD
US Postage Paid
Permit No. 6
Forks, WA

Change
Service
Requested

ECRWSS

Wednesday, January 30, 2008

www.forksforum.com

'Twilight' director eyes LaPush

Chris Cook photo

"Twilight" film director Catherine Hardwicke boards the Forks Chamber of Commerce's logging tours van Wednesday during a scouting trip to LaPush. Hardwicke is joined by Elliot Davis, the film's director of photography (center), and James Lin, the location director for the filming. At LaPush, below, the director looked over possible filming locations at the mouth of Lonesome Creek at First Beach with co-producer Jamie Marshall, left, and Davis. Logging tour driver Sonny Smith escorted the film crew.

by Chris Cook
Forks Forum editor

"Twilight" film director Catherine Hardwicke scouted First Beach at LaPush on Quileute Tribe lands on Wednesday for location filming of scenes planned for the upcoming screen version of the best-selling "Twilight" book series.

During her scouting at LaPush, Hardwicke said Kristen Stewart, who plays Isabella Swan, the lead female role in the film, and other actors would travel from Portland to film

See TWILIGHT, page 2

Future of Forks Aquatic Center pondered

by Chris Cook
Forks Forum editor

Forging a plan to somehow reopen the shuttered Forks Aquatic Center was the focus of a community meeting called last week by Mayor Nedra Reed and the Quillayute Valley Parks and Recreation District (QVPRD).

"What do we do now?" QVPRD boardmember Sandra Carter asked to open the meeting.

Voters rejected in November by a two-to-one margin the creation of a Metropolitan Park District with junior taxing authority that would have paid for the bulk of the annual cost of operating the pool located inside the aquatic center.

"The failure (of the election) caught me totally by surprise," Carter told the gathering. "I'm still willing to stick it out...I have hope for the future of the facility."

The pool and its building were opened in 2005 and paid for through a voter-approved bond issue that is being paid off into the 2020s.

The QVPRD was forced to close the pool in Sept. 2006 due to a lack of operating funds. The rising cost of propane needed to heat the pool, higher-than-estimated personnel pay and other factors were given as reasons for the closing.

Local residents and business people, and the two remaining board members of QVPRD spent

See POOL, page 3

ing the West End, Forks, LaPush, Beaver, Clallam Bay, Sekiu & Neah Bay since 1930

La Push was drop-dead gorgeous
but ultimately it cost too much to film there...

Question: How much is that deer head in the window?

Answer: A buck.

Everything is made of wood

Forks Coffee Shop
241 S. Forks Avenu
(PO Box 1804)
Forks, WA 98331
360-374-6769
www.forkscoffeeshop.c

Dinners

a garlic roll

od

$14
$14
$16
$11
$18
, clam stri

Chicken fried ste ...s	$13
Breaded veal	$11
***Liver and onion** ...oms	$11

Salads

Served with toast or a garlic roll

When I mentioned that I was working on a little movie called Twilight—all the hi-skoolers SCREAMED!

Desserts

...memade Pies		$3.
	Ala mode	$4.
Brownie Delight: a single brownie topped with ice cream, chocolate syrup and whipped cream		$4.
Berry Cobbler		$3.
	Ala mode	$4.
Ice Cream	Small	$1.
	Large	$2.
Sundaes: Choice of chocolate, strawberry, blackberry, pineapple, or butterscotch		$3.

I heard some of the locals ate here every night—so we sent Melissa the menu and she wrote the "diner" scenes. Berry cobbler came straight off their dessert list.

DIANE SHOSTAK AND HER FRIENDS GAVE US THE ROYAL TOUR OF FORKS !!!

WASHINGTON
FORKS
OLYMPIC PENINSULA

If you live in the Northwest, You gotta have a carved BEAR...

Kevin Rupprecht, the principal of Forks High, rolled out the welcome mat. We didn't end up shooting there for budget reasons, but they still helped us out with yearbooks, newspapers, letterman jackets—etc. Here's a big thanks.

VICTORIA JUMPS ONTO
THE BOAT!

I posed for this shot so I could draw a storyboard of Victoria.

CHARACTER DEVELOPMENT

DESIGNING THE HAIR, MAKE-UP, & COSTUMES

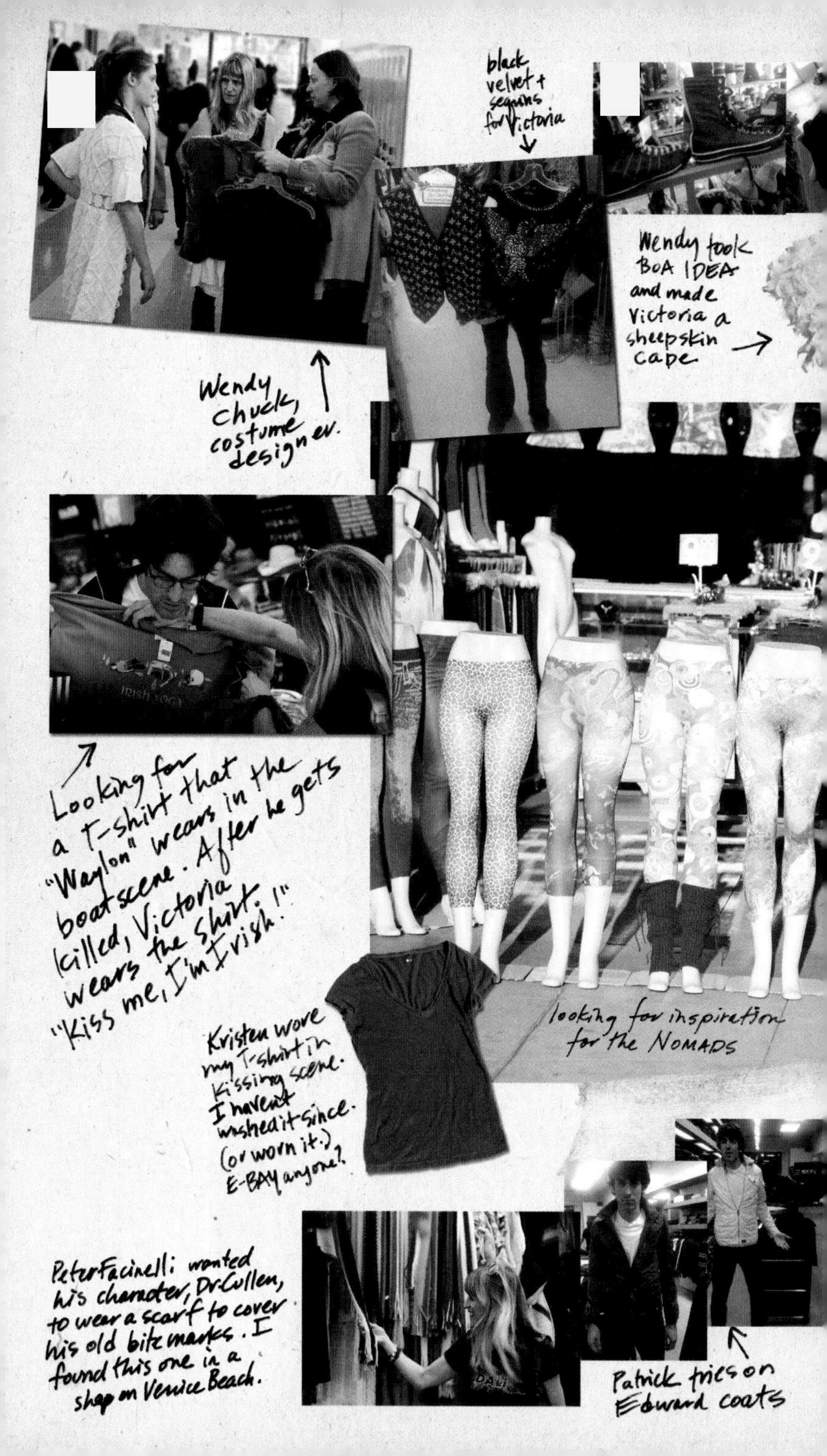
black velvet + sequins for Victoria
Wendy took BoA IDEA and made Victoria a sheepskin cape
Wendy Chuck, costume designer.
IRISH YOGA
Looking for a T-shirt that "Waylon" wears in the boat scene. After he gets killed, Victoria wears the shirt. "Kiss me, I'm Irish!"
looking for inspiration for the NOMADS
Kristen wore my T-shirt in kissing scene. I haven't washed it since. (or worn it.) E-BAY anyone?
Peter Facinelli wanted his character, Dr. Cullen, to wear a scarf to cover his old bite marks. I found this one in a shop on Venice Beach.
Patrick tries on Edward coats

Patrick Smith + Josh Lee (editorial P.A.) were forced into modeling possible wardrobe for the tribesmen
Alice? Baseball?
DALI
my Henry Duarte "rockstar" pants- worn by Victoria
HOSTEL
I had a 1940's Sears motorcycle jacket. This was the model for James' coat.
HUNTING & GATHERING IDEAS ...

Jeanne Van Phue, our make-up artist, had her friend Kathy Shorkey, do watercolors of the character looks. For Bella, Kristen has beautiful pale skin so we went with a very soft, natural look. To become Bella, Kristen wears brown contacts.

The first challenge for me was to find the perfect Bella. Stephenie created a 17-yr-old with a quiet courage — but a capacity for profound love. I had seen Kristen Stewart's brief but powerful performance in "Into the Wild" and I was impressed with her depth and vulnerability. When she is sitting on the bed in the trailer, her intense yearning and desire was palpable.

So I flew to Pittsburgh where Kristen was filming "Adventureland." On Sunday, her one day off, we rehearsed several scenes and ended up chasing pigeons in the park. When I reviewed the video the next day in LA, I knew I'd found Bella Swan.

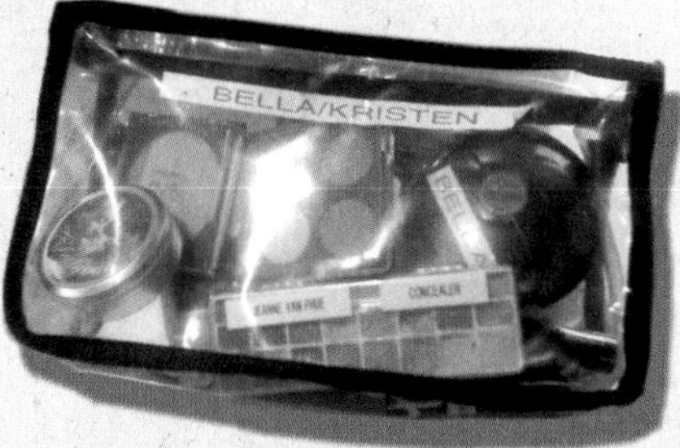

Mary Ann Valdes, hair designer, supervised the dyeing of Kristen's hair — to a deep, chestnut brown with hi-lites. To thicken it up, she made a hairpiece that was laid under Kristen's hair. Kristen also wears a headband frequently to prevent the "Cousin It" look.

Bella's Wardrobe

Wendy Chuck, our costume designer, worked with illustrator Oksana Nedavniaya, to create Bella's "look."

Bella starts out more "tomboy" and covered up— bulky coats etc.

BELLA'S COLOR PALETTE

EARTHTONES

END OF FILM

BLUE JACKET IN BALLET STUDIO

MORE LIKE CULLENS

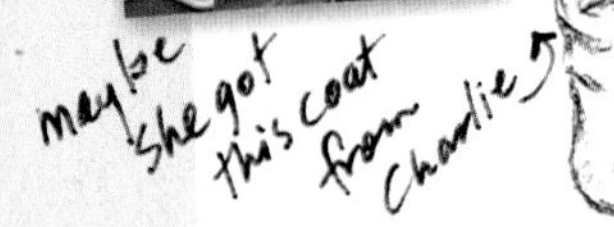

maybe she got this coat from Charlie?

shirt was re-made in "forest green" for first day of school.

Character Arc:
As Bella falls
in love, she
starts to dress
a little more
feminine...
floral prints,
more formfitting, etc...
Kristen
liked a
couple of
pairs of my shoes -
cuz they were
worn in
too cold
to go sleeveless
so Wendy found
this vintage
sweater in
Portland

Edward

Robert Pattinson

Out of thousands of actors submitted to our casting directors, I met with dozens of guys. They were all good-looking, but they mostly felt like they were the boy next door—not an otherworldly vampire. I was getting worried—everybody wanted the perfect Edward. I spoke to Rob on the phone in London, but I needed to see him in person. His agent convinced him to fly out to L.A. and sleep on her couch. He came to my house, along with 3 other "semi-finalists" and auditioned with Kristen. When they did the "kissing scene" on my bed—well, let's just say that Rob got the part.

Kathy's original watercolor of Edward with long hair and brown contacts. I thought he would look good with long "timeless" hair, so Rob spent 8 hours in the chair—Nicole Frank, assistant hair stylist—put in extensions. Rob HATED them. The next day Nicole yanked them out and she and MaryAnn and Rob started working on the now-famous Edward hairstyle.

CASTING REQUIREMENTS:
- PALE SKIN
- LOOKS LIKE HE IS 17
- GREAT ACTOR
- GREAT CHEMISTRY W/ KRISTEN
- BEST LOOKING GUY IN THE WORLD

Yea, Rob looks good in anything...

As soon as Rob was cast, he moved to Oregon and began working on his character – both mentally and physically. He worked out 5 hours a day with a trainer – learning to fight, to play baseball, and do stunts. (He even had to learn to drive and get an Oregon drivers license.) Emotionally, he started thinking deeply about Edward – his feelings of anger, love, regret, loneliness – what it felt like to struggle as Edward does.

Wendy made a shorter version of a classic pea jacket in light gray (not traditional vampire black) for the signature "Edward jacket"

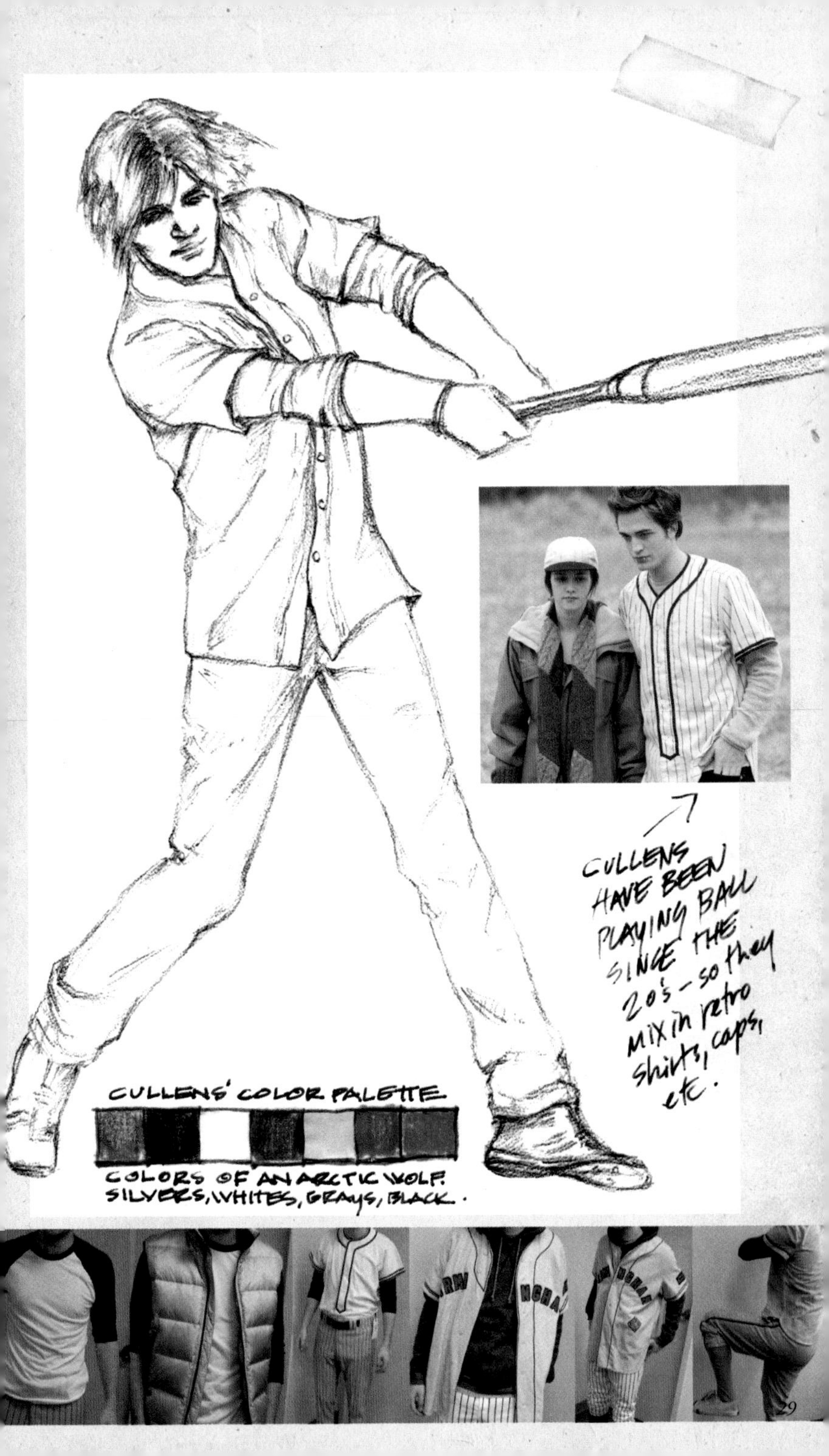
CULLENS HAVE BEEN PLAYING BALL SINCE THE 20's - so they mix in retro shirts, caps, etc.
CULLENS' COLOR PALETTE
COLORS OF AN ARCTIC WOLF. SILVERS, WHITES, GRAYS, BLACK.

Ashley wore a wig-
we kept cutting it
shorter until we
got it right.
Hungry dark eyes
Golden eyes - full

NOTE: IN THE BOOK, ALL THE CULLENS HAVE LIGHT GOLDEN EYES WHEN THEY ARE FULL, AND BLACK EYES WHEN THEY ARE HUNGRY. THIS MEANT THAT NEARLY EVERY ACTOR HAD TO WEAR CONTACT LENSES.

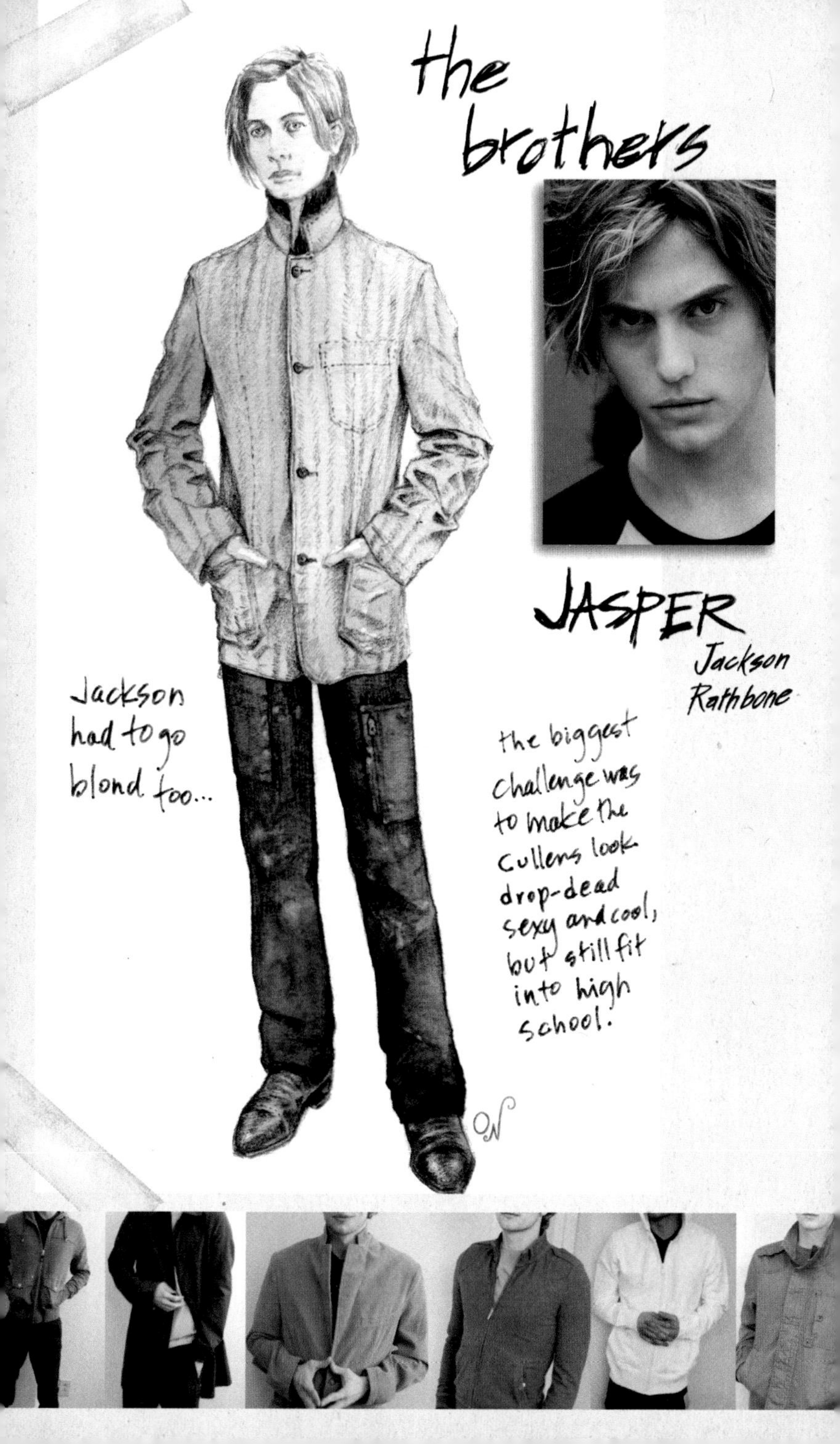
the brothers
JASPER
Jackson Rathbone
Jackson had to go blond too...
the biggest challenge was to make the Cullens look drop-dead sexy and cool, but still fit into high school.

Nikki is right-handed— here she is at a costume fitting at Universal studios. She learned how to bat left-handed because I thought I was going to shoot her from the right side. . . . oops . . . .

Rosalie

Nikki Reed

I've known Nikki since she was 5 years old. At age 13, she and I co-wrote "Thirteen" and she starred in it. When I read Twilight, I thought Nikki would be perfect for Rosalie. She's unafraid to speak her mind. When I called her to talk about the part, she said "Everyone will want Bella & Edward to be together. Rosalie is trying to break them up – so they'll hate me. I'm ok with that."

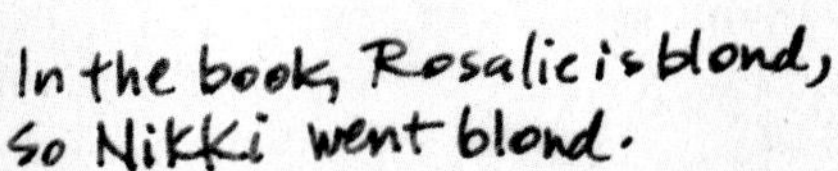
In the book, Rosalie is blond, so Nikki went blond.

Alice
Ashley Greene
In Chapter 22 of Twilight, we
find out that Alice was confined
to a mental hospital in the '20s.
So her hair was cut off
jagged—SHORT & SPIKY.
Stressed Out?
COUNSELING
WALK-INS WELCOME
we wanted
all of Alice's
clothes to
have a touch
of magic.

EMMETT Kellan Lutz
medium blue velour
INDIGO NAVY
white stripe
grey/silver velour
No retro shirt for Emmett— the superjock wore a velour track suit

Dr. Carlisle Cullen
Peter Facinelli
Peter did a great audition but another actor was originally offered the part. So Peter bought a cool vampire book and sent it to me with a great letter, saying "I hope we get to work together another time." When the other actor's schedule didn't work out, I looked at the book and said:
"Let's hire Peter." He jokes that he spent $29.95 to get the job.
Peter had to dye his hair blond too—

Esme
Elizabeth Reaser
It was so cold we had to add gloves and a coat to Esme's baseball costume

The Cullen Crest

Oksana drew variations
I had this pendant which we used as a model
Cynthia Nibler, our propmaster, refined the designs
A
B
the HAND = faith, sincerity
the LION = strength, ferocity
the TREFOIL = perpetuity

Wendy Chuck had the idea that the Cullens could have some kind of a family crest—"clan jewelry."

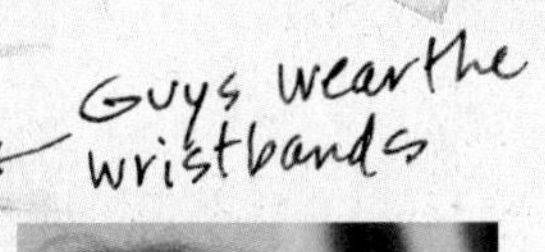

Guys wear the wristbands

Rosalie wears the pendant

Alice—choker

In her audition, Rachelle climbed over the chair & hissed at me like a mad tigress.

Laurent Edi Gathegi

Edi rocked a dreads wig and Edwardian threads. He hit the gym in the Portland Hotel so he could go bare-chested.

These guys are NOT vegetarians- eyes always RED.
(But the hand-painted red contacts were painful ... suffering for ART...

Victoria look #1 ↓

70's vintage jacket ↓

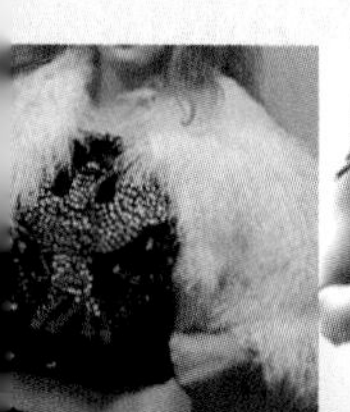

Victoria
Rachelle Lefevre

Look #1

JAMES
Cam Gigandet

CAM'S JEANS WERE DISTRESSED ROCK-STAR STYLE—SANDED IN KNEES AND CROTCH.

JAMES COLLECTS TROPHIES FROM HIS VICTIMS. NOTE: SECURITY GUARD BADGE FROM GRISHAM MILL KILL SCENE.

James drains Waylon's blood, then he takes his jacket.

Look #2

Waylon
Ned Bellamy

THE NOMADS

Victoria snags Waylon's "Kiss Me I'm Irish" T-shirt.

Look #2

JACOB BLACK AND THE QUILEUTES

Taylor Lautner

GIL BIRMINGHAM AKA "BILLY BLACK" WORE HIS OWN TRIBAL JACKET.

JACOB ROCKS A CASUAL "NOT TRYING TOO HARD" LOOK

taylor had to wear a WIG—NOT HIS FAVORITE THANG.

Krystopher Hyatt, local Portland skateboarder. He and Soloman already had looooong hair.

SOLOMON TRIMBLE, AKA "JACOB'S FRIEND," WEARS A JACKET HIS MOM MADE OUT OF A WOLF/SHAPESHIFTER PENDLETON BLANKET.

The HUMANS

Anna Kendrick aka "Jessica" impressed me with her comic timing as a speed-talking debater in the Sundance favorite "Rocket Science."

Mike Welch aka "Mike" sports a real Letterman jacket from Forks High school.

TRIVIA POINT: NAME BELLA'S PAL. HINT: SHE IS IDENTIFIED ELSEWHERE IN THIS BOOK AND IS A MODEL IN A GLOBAL MARKETING CAMPAIGN.

Justin Chon, aka "Eric" showed up in Portland without his cool "audition" shirt and tie. I said "can't your roommate send it to you? I mean, that's why I hired you, dude."

For Anna, of course we had to pick the prom dress that made her boobs look good.

Christian Serratos, AKA "Angela," wore her own geek chic glasses

HOT TIP FOR ACTORS: DRESS FOR THE PART!

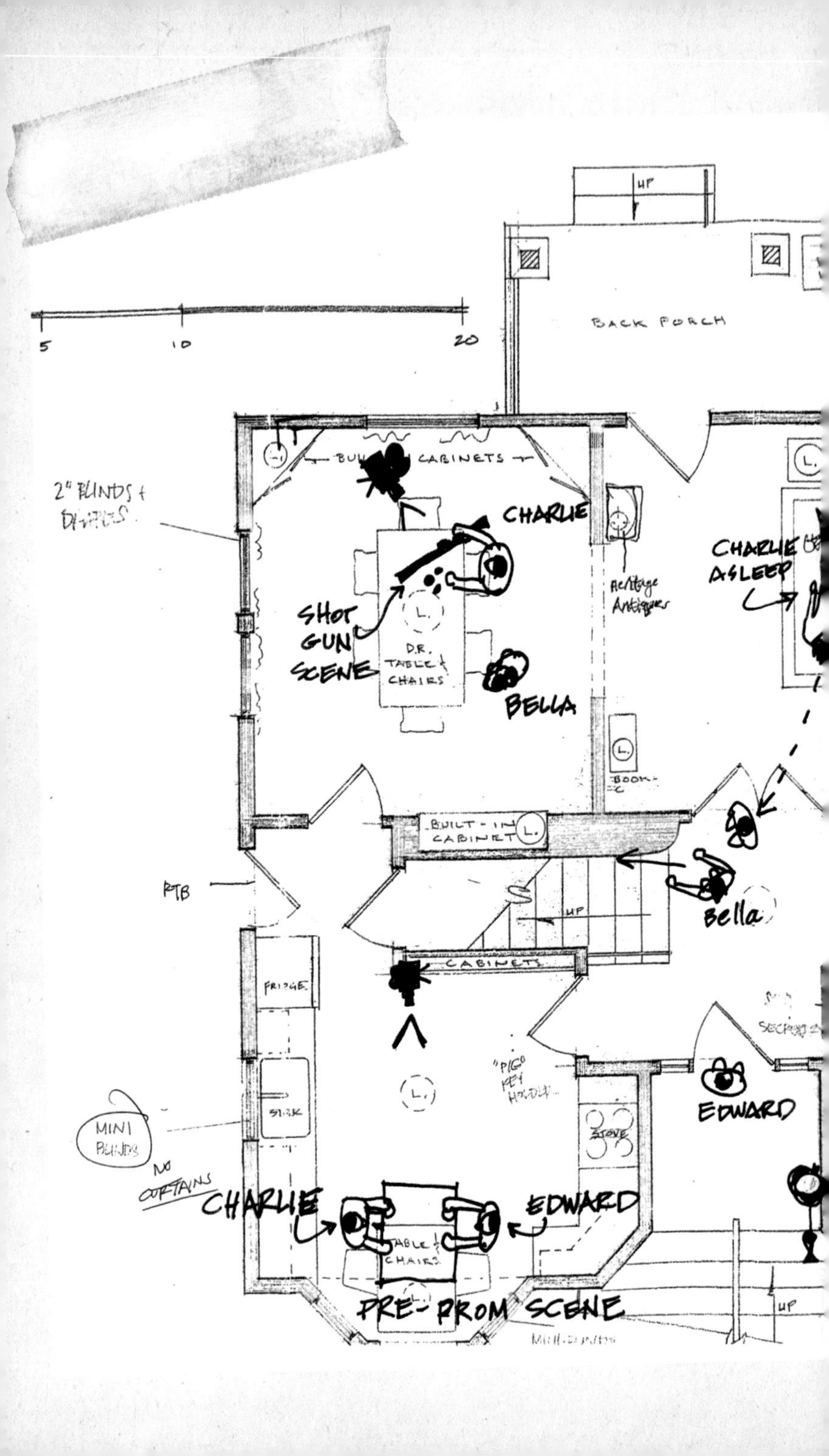

UP
BACK PORCH
5
10
20
CABINETS
CHARLIE
SHOT GUN SCENE
D.R. TABLE + CHAIRS
BELLA
CHARLIE ASLEEP
BUILT-IN CABINET
Bella
UP
CABINETS
FRIDGE
SINK
"PIG" KEY HOLDER
STOVE
EDWARD
MINI BLINDS
NO CURTAINS
CHARLIE
EDWARD
TABLE + CHAIRS
PRE-PROM SCENE
UP

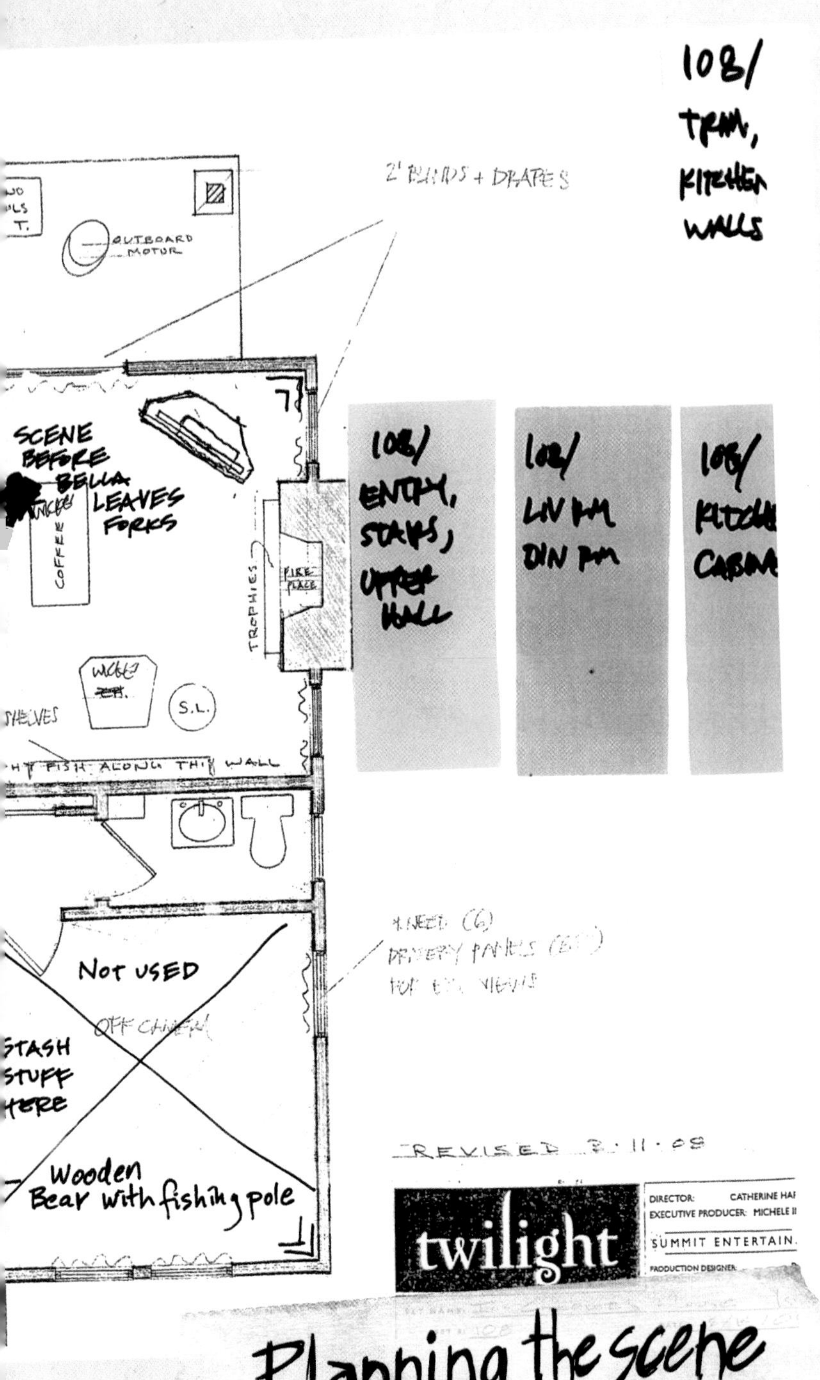
108/
TRIM,
KITCHEN
WALLS
2' BLINDS + DRAPES
OUTBOARD
MOTOR
SCENE
BEFORE
BELLA
LEAVES
FORKS
COFFEE
TROPHIES
FIRE
PLACE
S.L.
SHELVES
FISH ALONG THIS WALL
108/
ENTRY,
STAIRS,
UPPER
HALL
108/
LIV RM
DIN RM
108/
Not USED
OFF CAMERA
STASH
STUFF
HERE
Wooden
Bear with fishing pole
REVISED 3 · 11 · 08
twilight
DIRECTOR:
EXECUTIVE PRODUCER:
SUMMIT ENTERTAIN.
PRODUCTION DESIGNER:

Planning the scene

CHARLIE'S HOUSE

paper towels, solo cups—
more "big box" supplies

C Hardwicke Note
"pig-shaped"
key holder!

"Before" Kitchen with
Gene Serdena (the set decorator)
Notes

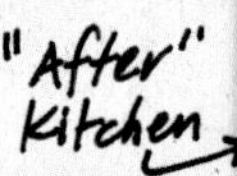

"After"
Kitchen

"BEFORE" LIVING ROOM

"AFTER" LIVING ROOM

one of the first things you often do when you film in a house is PAINT the ~~tall~~ white walls darker. You can't easily control the light if it is bouncing off big white surfaces. Rich colors also add to the mood and character of the place.

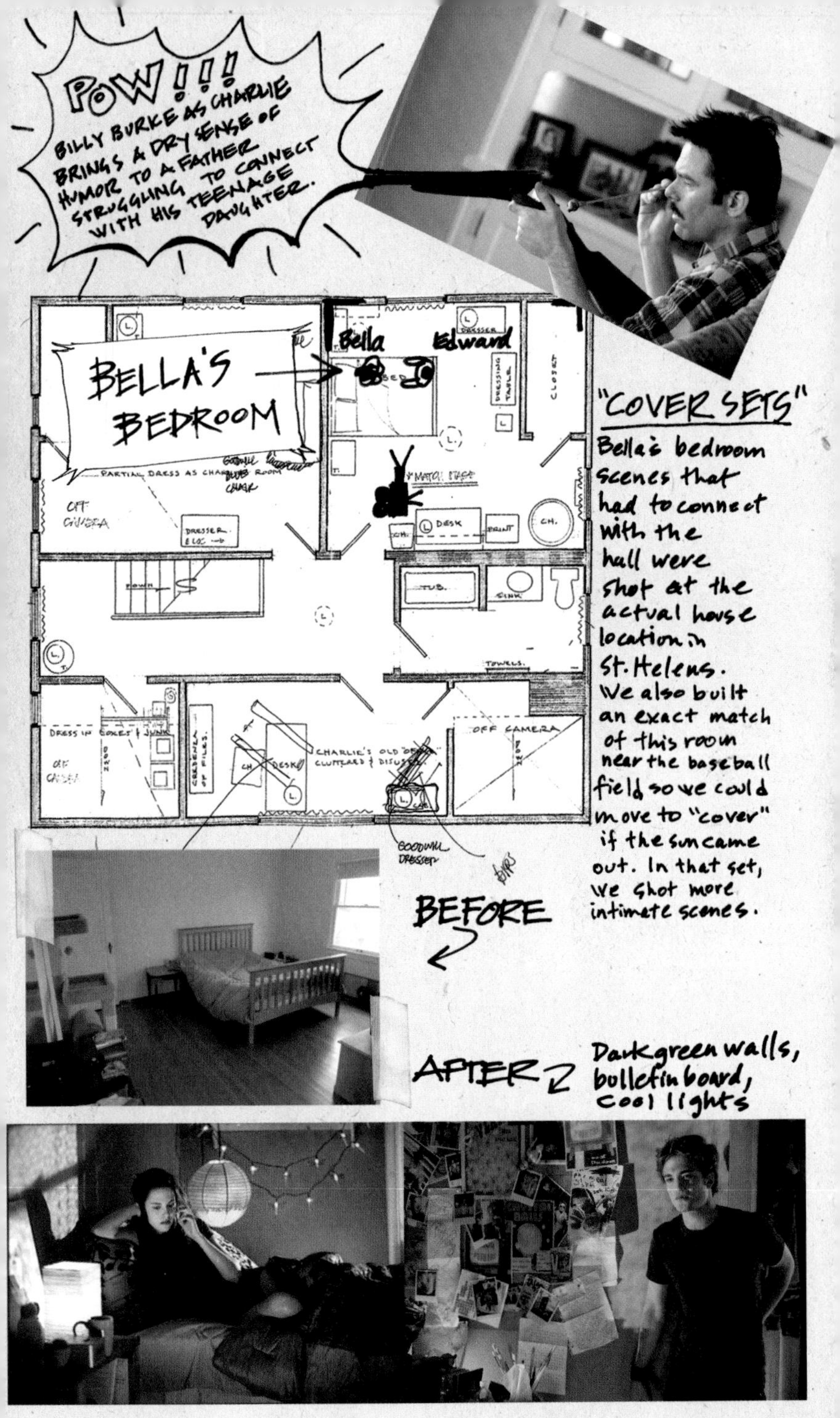

POW!!!
BILLY BURKE AS CHARLIE BRINGS A DRY SENSE OF HUMOR TO A FATHER STRUGGLING TO CONNECT WITH HIS TEENAGE DAUGHTER.
BELLA'S BEDROOM
Bella
Edward
DRESSER
DRESSING TABLE
CLOSET
PARTIAL DRESS AS CHARLIE'S ROOM
OFF CAMERA
DRESSER
DESK
CH.
TUB.
SINK
TOWELS.
DOWN
DRESS IN BOXES & JUNK
CREDENZA OF FILES.
CHARLIE'S OLD DESK CLUTTERED & DISUSED
OFF CAMERA
"COVER SETS"
Bella's bedroom scenes that had to connect with the hall were shot at the actual house location in St. Helens. We also built an exact match of this room near the baseball field so we could move to "cover" if the sun came out. In that set, we shot more intimate scenes.
BEFORE
AFTER
Dark green walls, bulletin board, cool lights

I wanted to make Edward's internal conflict visual—so he jerks away violently from Bella when her scent is too strong. Stunt double Paul Darnell gets yanked across the room on a wire rig. He's wearing a safety harness under his T-shirt. We removed the wire digitally.

This 3 part montage showed Edward staying over with Bella, watching her sleep...

...struggling to be this close to her without killing her...

Spot the Differences

THIS SCENE WAS ORIGINALLY SHOT IN OREGON. WE GOT "SUNNED OUT" WHILE FILMING THE BASEBALL SCENE. A FREAK WEEK OF WINTER SUN! SO WE BUILT BELLA'S BEDROOM IN A SHED AND ONLY HAD A FEW HOURS TO SHOOT THE KISSING SCENE. AND KRISTEN HAD TO GO TO "SCHOOL" BETWEEN SHOTS.

RESULT: I DIDN'T GET TO SHOOT THE "STUNT" OR EDWARD STAYING OVERNITE. AND I KNEW WE COULD MAKE THE KISS BETTER. SO IN AUGUST, WE RE-SHOT THIS SCENE ON A SET IN AN ELKS LODGE IN PASADENA. THIS TIME, KRISTEN WAS 18!

be very still...
don't move

creating
ARIZONA
Anybody know how to fly this bird?
N67TV
ADD PALM TREES
AND CACTI
I went to phoenix for a day to do aerial shots
I wanted Bella to take a little piece of Arizona with her...

We had to shoot this scene in Valencia, CA. for budgetary reasons. I chose this location for the expansive view at the end of the street. I thought it could be a "poetic" opening.

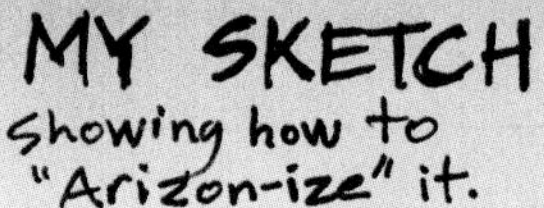

MY SKETCH
showing how to "Arizon-ize" it.

Rent-a-cactus
DON'T TRY THIS AT HOME.

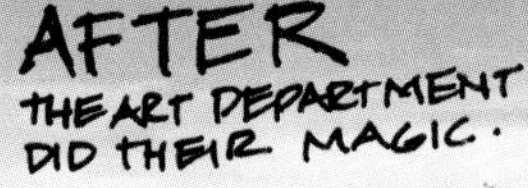

AFTER
THE ART DEPARTMENT DID THEIR MAGIC.

the other neighbors were bummed that they didn't get a free paint job

CAFETERIA

TRIVIA NOTE: WHEN ROB ENTERS THE CAFETERIA, HIS REAL LIFE SISTER, LIZZIE PATTINSON, SINGS VOCALS ON THE SOUND TRACK....
EDWARD'S ENTRANCE
HUMAN'S TABLE
Look, I designed this really cool salad for you, Kristen.
WOW.
SALAD BAR
yes, I really designed this "edible art." Feel free to use it to pick up hot guys at salad bars.

SHOCKING!!!
ELECTRIFYING!!!

ATTACK OF THE GIANT

we tried about 10 times to get the apple shot—the clock was ticking—I started thinking this was a really dumb idea. I almost gave up—but we got it on TAKE 13... my lucky number.

Stephenie Meyer and Summit CEO Rob Friedman visit the set.

Is that a TV around your Neck?

I'm wearing a monitor so I can watch the exact camera shots and still stand close to the actors—NOT BACK at "VIDEO VILLAGE."

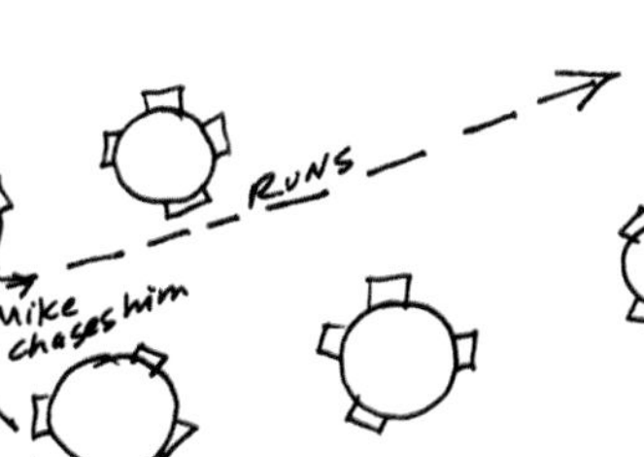

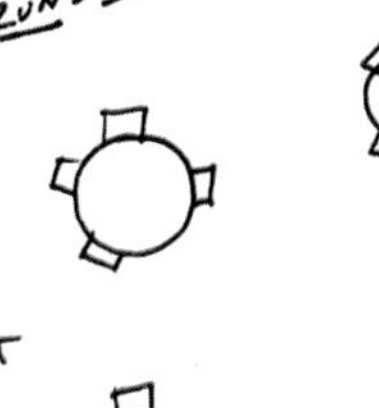

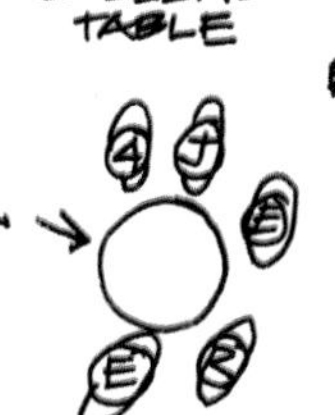

CULLENS' TABLE—BACKLIT AGAINST the WINDOW FOR MAXIMUM DRAMA

LIGHTING BLIMP!!!

WOLF LEGENDS

Susan Matheson, our costume designer for the "ADDITIONAL PHOTOGRAPHY" IN AUGUST, came up with the CULLENS' 1930's hunting clothes and the tribes men's wardrobe.

WAIT A MINUTE. WHAT'S MY MOTIVATION?

Propmaster Cynthia Nibler had wolf masks made. Challenge: FIND A FOTO IN THIS BOOK of the Nibler holding a wolf mask.

DO WOLVES REALLY PREFER BLONDES?

I loved the all-female wolf trainers - we've come a long way since Little Red Riding Hood, baby...

River's Edge

TWILIGHT PARADOX:
WHEN THE SUN CAME OUT,
WE MADE RAIN.

AS A SUN "COVERSET", I SAW THIS AREA ON THE BACKSIDE OF THE MOSSY ROCKS—IT WOULD BE IN SHADE IN THE AFTERNOONS, SO WE MADE A "RAIN CAVE" WITH FAKE RAIN SO WE COULD KEEP FILMING AFTER THE SUN CAME OUT.

I fell in love with this location overlooking the Columbia River. When co-producer Jamie Marshall and I sat in for Bella & Edward, I had no idea how difficult it would be to film here. The moss was so fragile that even one footstep destroyed it and it was so slippery that one false move would plunge someone into HYPOTHERMIA—so...

...Platforms were constructed by Steve Smith's Grip Department. This large platform had to be removed in 15 minutes to get a clean wide "Beauty shot" before the sun came out.

the CULLEN HOUSE

It looked like a treehouse...

Beth Melnick, our Portland location scout found this amazing new house—just built by a marketing executive—We took all their valuable artwork out for safe-keeping...

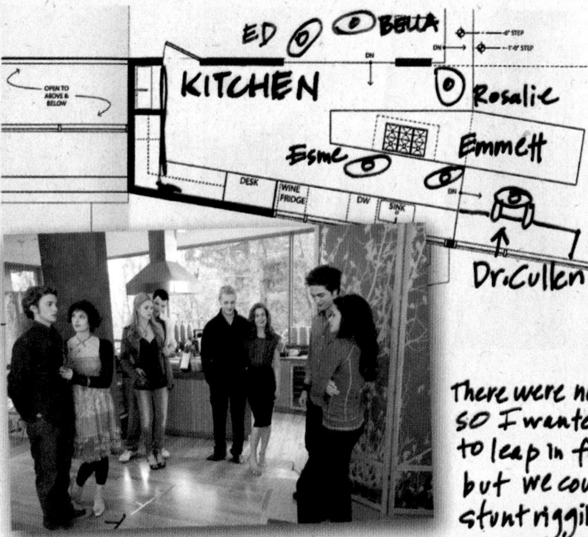

There were no stairs like the book, so I wanted Alice + Jasper to leap in from a tree—but we couldn't afford the stunt rigging.

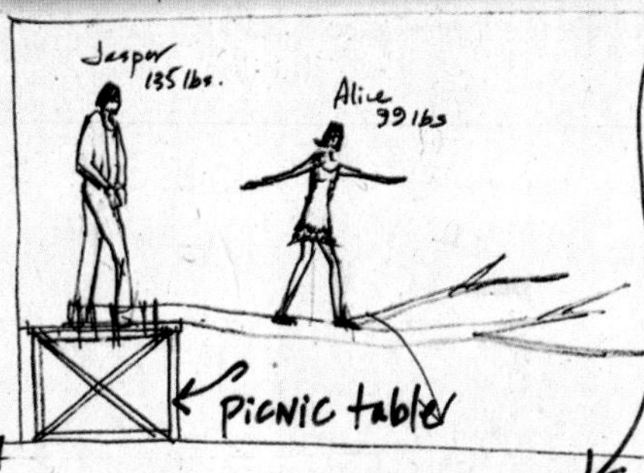

So I drew this diagram and said "NAIL A BRANCH TO A PICNIC TABLE AND PUT IT ON THE BALCONY AND WE'LL DO IT FOR FREE"—(almost)

Before ⟶ this bedroom actually had a door opening to nowhere... perfect...

No bed?

Set decorators put in a music collection—CD's, vinyl, 8-tracks, 78's, old Victrolas, radios, global musical instruments....

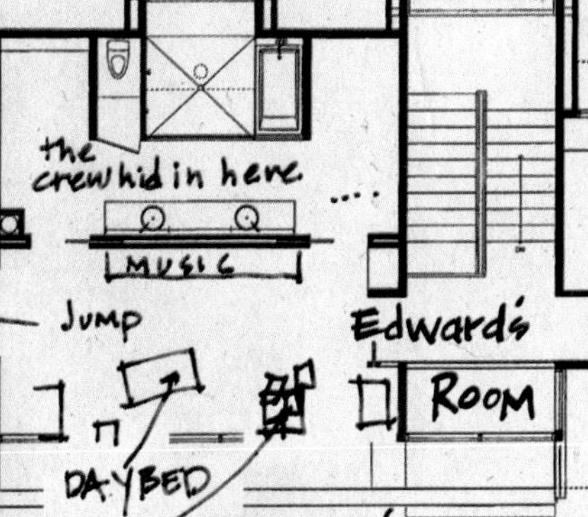

100 years of journals

I came up with the idea of a "color field" collage art piece made of graduation caps as a visual way to show that the Cullens had been to lots of high skools. Set decoration department made it. Also the collection of old baseball bats.

Graduation caps?

DRIVING SHOTS

WIDE/STUNT DOUBLES

3

NITE #103 + #104pt
TRUCK - PROCESS TRAILER #1

#103
2
Bella looks at Edward (TP)

#103
1 RAKING
1A BELLA #104 LOOKS AT COFFEE SHOP - AND INNOCENT FRIENDS

Emmett jumps into back

3

DRIVING SHOTS =
• LOTS of EQUIPMENT
• LOTS of RIGGING
• LOTS of PLANNING
AAAGH....

PROCESS TRAILER #1

ANGELES
EST FOREST

BELLA'S TRUCK - EDWARD TAKES THE WHEEL

7/8 page SC. 103 - NITE - WOODS -

Kellan did his own stunts - it was fun until the 10th time at 30° at 2AM. He said "Uh, I'm a little cold."

tick, tock!

Kristen was 17 when we started filming & state laws limit the amount of time a minor can work. So all the complex nite scenes had to wait. Her birthday cake had a big icing clock and said: "WELCOME to NITES!"

The Volvo is mounted onto a process trailer. We shot down Main Street in St. Helens after midnite.

the PROM

EUREKA MOMENT: I shot this photo of misty green hills and thought — move the prom out of the gym — make it outside — romantic… dreamy… so I sketched the prom tent into the corner. We found an Inn with a view of the river.

Eureka Moment #2: The Inn had a bedroom overlooking the view — so we ended the film with Victoria watching Edward & Bella — plotting her revenge.

JUST ADD FOG

We shot a new scene in August where Jacob comes to prom to warn Bella. Amazingly, we found a house in Pasadena that matched our Oregon location.

BEFORE

the art department built a GAZEBO with a rotating turntable and a clear plastic roof.

AFTER

Elliot Davis, our cinematographer, had a vision of a magical world — which required literally hundreds of white lights. We kept adding more and more and more...

the VAN CRASH

Tech Scout

Technical department heads from 1st and 2nd Unit, Art Dept., Transportation, stunts, special FX, visual FX – planning the shots.

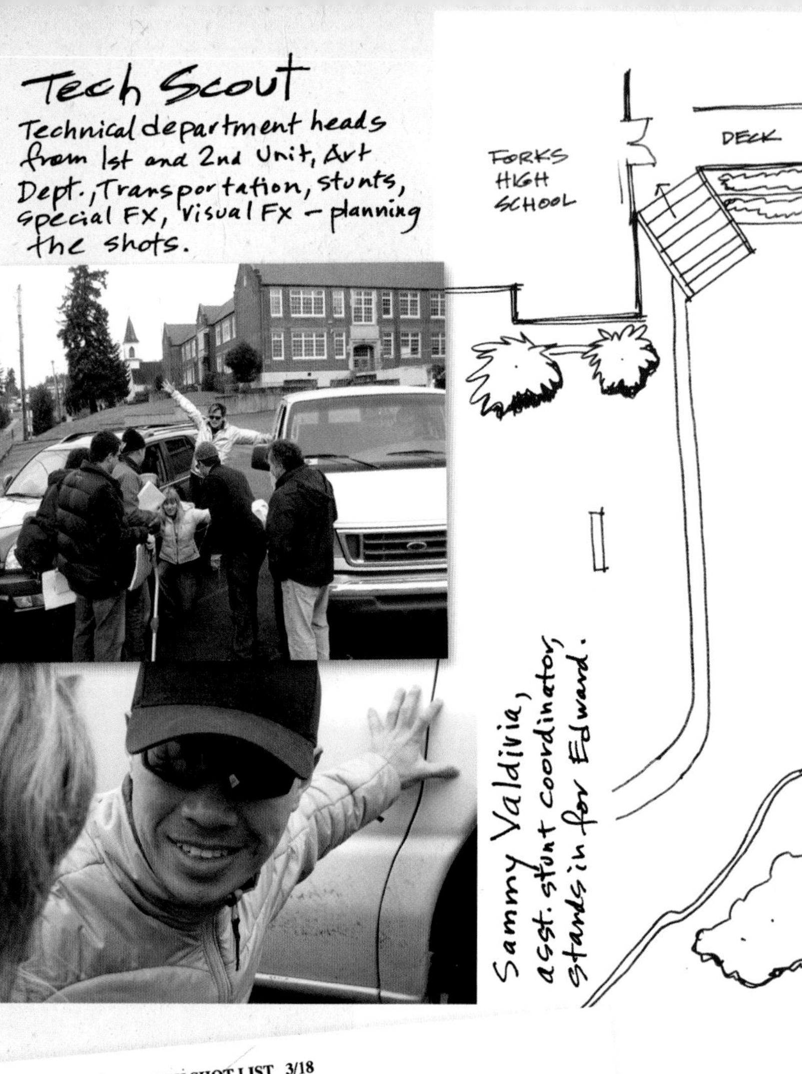

Sammy Valdivia, asst. stunt coordinator, stands in for Edward.

KALAMA HIGH SHOT LIST 3/18

Sc. 19 & 20 PARKING LOT – Bella exits 1st Day of School

1. STEADICAM back with Bella, heading downstairs past Cullens at their cars, to her truck.
2. INSIDE TRUCK: Bella upset.

CU Rob

Sc. 67 LAWN – Bella confronts Edward

1. WIDE MASTER STEADICAM OTS. Bella's shoulder as she watches students running to classes. Edward enters frame and sees Bella staring. He stops. STEADICAM follows her approaching him, giving him a "LOOK... walk right past him into the WIDE ENOUGH to see the Cullens enter, and lets Bella ... woods.

1a. Single on EDWARD as she approaches, then staring at her, turning to go after Bella.

2. LOOKING TOWARD SCHOOL: STEADICAM ON BELLA as people rush around her. She spots Edward – then STEADICAM leads her back as she determinedly walks forward and stops to confront Edward.

3. PROFILE: TWO SHOT of Bella stepping up to face Edward, then crossing past him. He turns and follows her, leaving siblings staring..

Covered in a diff. w

#53 SUNNY DAY

on deck near front entry or in back "yard" near gym.

... on picnic table. ON DOLLY: Tight on BELLA looking around for Edward, pull ... then Angela bursts in . THREE SHOT

I made shot lists for every scene.

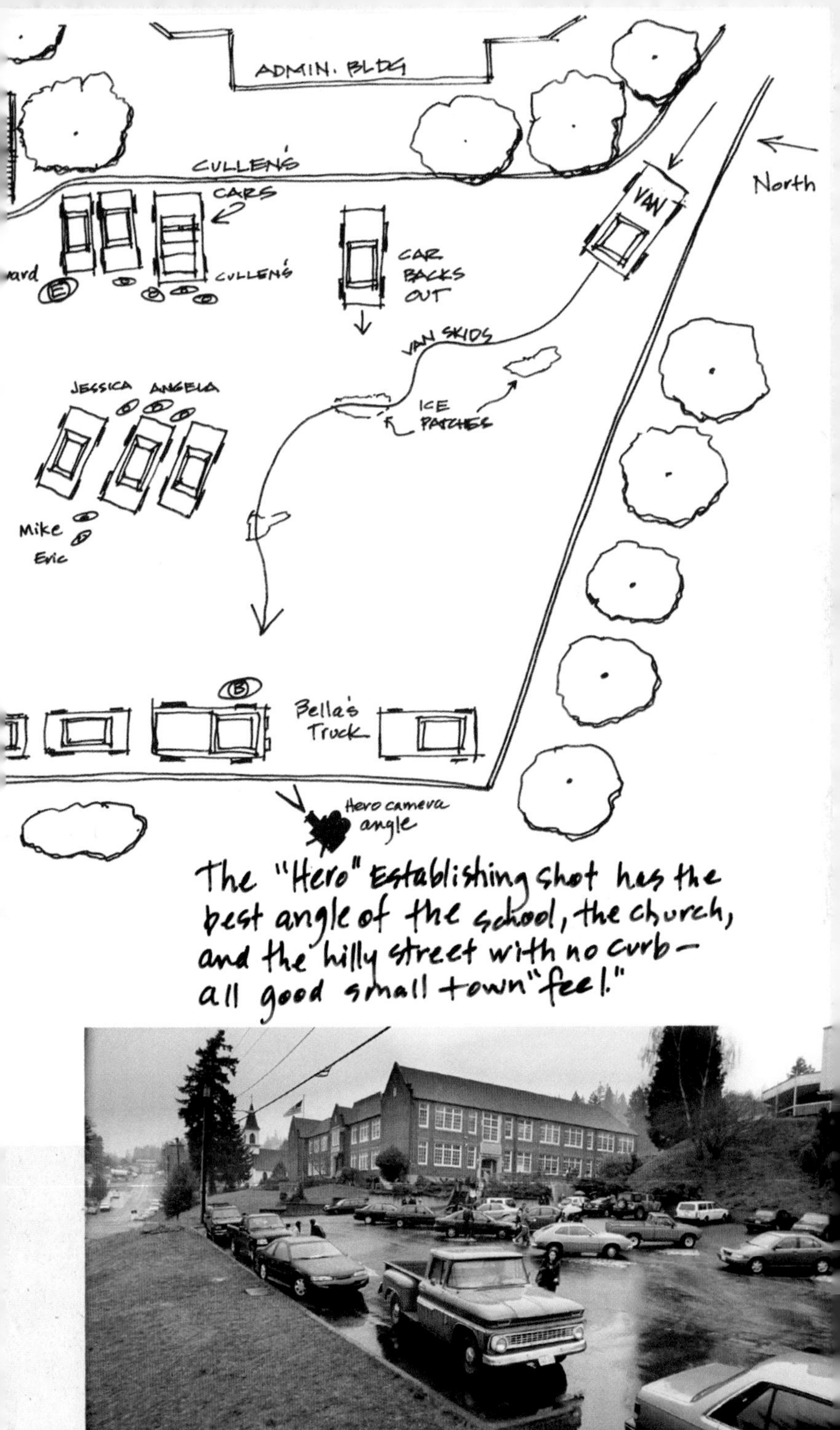
ADMIN. BLDG
CULLEN'S CARS
North
VAN
CAR BACKS OUT
E
CULLEN'S
VAN SKIDS
ICE PATCHES
JESSICA
ANGELA
Mike
Eric
B
Bella's Truck
Hero camera angle
The "Hero" Establishing shot has the best angle of the school, the church, and the hilly street with no curb—all good small town "feel."

... REVEAL BELLA
TILT & BOOM -UP
LEADING GIRL WALKING ACROSS PARKING LOT...

It was important to establish that Edward was on the other side of the parking lot—nowhere near Bella.

TRACK
90° PAN
TRACK BEHIND BELLA ACROSS LOT; SHE GLANCES OVER TO SIDE - PAN W/ HER GAZE TO FIND EDWARD W/FAMILY AT THEIR CAR.

CAM
CAM
Philip Keller drew some great storyboards for the Forks High School parking lot. Unfortunately, they did not fit the geography of Kalama High School, where we ended up filming.
PAN

CAM
CAM
TRANS
SLO-MO
... & STARTS
TO FISHTAIL.
Gregory Tyree Boyce
aka
TYLER
9
CLOSER P.O.V.-
WHEELS SLIDE
ON VAN

VAN CRASH SHOT LIST Jan. 11, 2009/CH

Non-Bella shots. CLOUDY!

my morning beet juice

1. WIDE EST. Bella heading to truck (board #1)
1a. B Cam – tight Bella (bd. #3, #5a)

2. OTS Bella to Cullens (bd #2) COULD USE BELLA DOUBLES
2a. B Cam – tight on Cullens. (bd #4, 7 car backs up) Bella's POV of Ed.
~~(bd. #A8 – Tyler driving, reacting)~~

I love that band

3. Tyler's POV skidding toward Bella (bd #10)
3a. B CAM tight on Bella. (bd #11)

4. Med. Bella – Ed rushes in & pushes her out of way. (bd#13A)

board

5. LOW ANGLE – Bella falls to ground (bd #14)

6. COMBINE INTO TWO SHOT for more Romantic Moment (redraw bd.#16a,17, 18. 19)
6a. B Cam – tight on Bella,
6b. B CAM – tight on Edward reacting to van.

10. SLIDING RIG SHOT – Multiple cameras – van on rig- i

11. Shot on Ed breathing hard, pan down to Bella (bd #23)

12. Bella's POV of Ed – dented van in BG (bd #25)

13. Pan down to Ed looking up (bd #26) (fix)
~~14. Coverage on Bella looking confused (bd #27)~~

VAN CRASH SECOND UNIT

—talk to Andy don't need overhead

1. WIDE – car backs up, starts the Van fishtail (bd #8)
1a. B CAM - close on Van wheels sliding. 2)
2. Bella double turns and sees van sliding toward her. C
2a. Continuation of OVERHEAD shot. (bd #22)
3. HI WIDE GEOGRAPHY showing ~~kids~~ running in. (bd #28)
4. Bella's POV – Edward touches her (bd #15)
5. Over Edward as van fills frame for impact. (bd. #2

No, I don't secretly want to be Bella. The storyboard artist was long gone by this time, so we did photoboards—as the only female, I had to stand in for Bella—

You stopped the van.

Andy's team made removable soft metal panels with plasticine backings that molded into the shape of Rob's hand on impact.

Andy Weder, our Special Effects Coordinator, stripped the engine out of a "stunt van", then rigged it on small "skateboard" wheels onto a SLIDE RIG. This way, the stopping point could be controlled for actors' safety. At impact, an air ram is activated so the van "jerks" to a stop.

"SKATE" WHEELS
REMOVED DIGITALLY

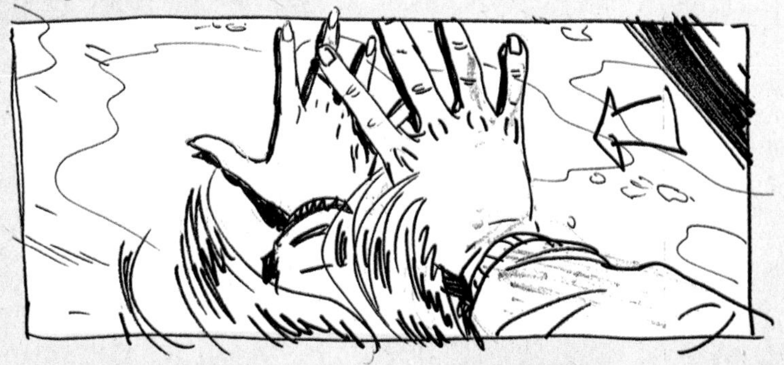

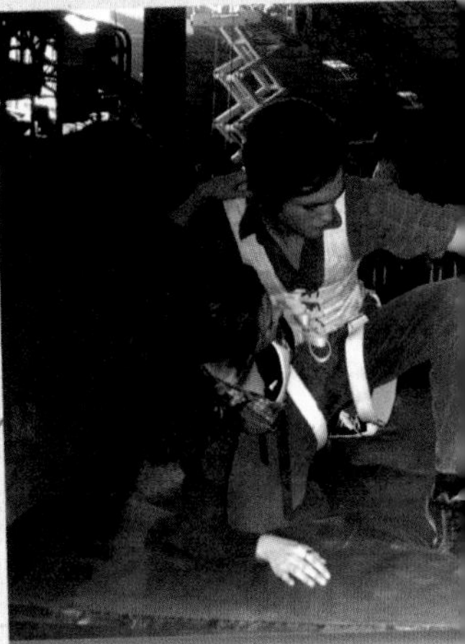

1. Asst. stunt coordinator Sammy Valdivia and I figured out action and final positions on the tech scout. Note: the "Hero" angle of the school lines up between the vehicles.

2. Kristen and Rob, wearing a safety harness, rehearse the moves at the warehouse.

Key frame by Philip Keller

(3.) Bella and Edward on the shoot day repeat the action. Positions had to be precise to match 2nd Unit, which was shot afterward. The distance from the car had to be precisely pre-planned for the sliding van stunt rig so no one would be injured — and Rob's hand had to line up with the replacement van door panel.

THE MEADOW

Our first day in Portland, location scout Don Baldwin took us to Oxbow Park. It was love at first sight.

Moss, Mist, Magic

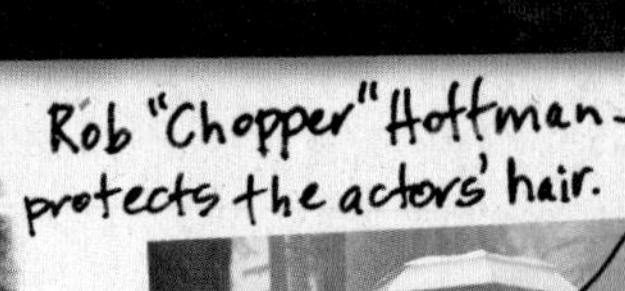

Rob "Chopper" Hoffman protects the actors' hair.

How long have you been 17?

Awhile.

We used a technocrane and a steadicam to get the sweeping, hypnotic shots . . .

Gaffer JIM GILSON takes a light reading

1. We had a spectacular location near the Salmon River — with a huge prehistoric rock for the big "sunlight" reveal. Trevor Goring storyboarded the whole sequence — great drawings with darkness and light — high contrast chiaroscuro effect...

2. JAMIE scheduled the meadow at the end of the shoot so the grass would be green and the leaves would be happy. But alas, it was not meant to be. Spring came late in 2008....

snow monkeys did this.

3. the location was still under snow at the end of April
@!?@!

4. Beth Melnick came up with an emergency solution — a moss-covered abandoned stone quarry. Logistically difficult, but drop dead gorgeous.
5. Most of the storyboards were now irrelevant — so I went out on Sunday to the new location and re-blocked it with our doubles — Logan Welch & Katie Powers.
2ND UNIT STUNT DOUBLES PAUL DARNELL & HELENA BARRETT ARE PULLED BY CABLE RIGS IN REMOTE LOCATION, SILVER SPRINGS.

1st unit couldn't go to Silver Springs, so this is one of only 2 GREEN SCREEN shots in the whole film.

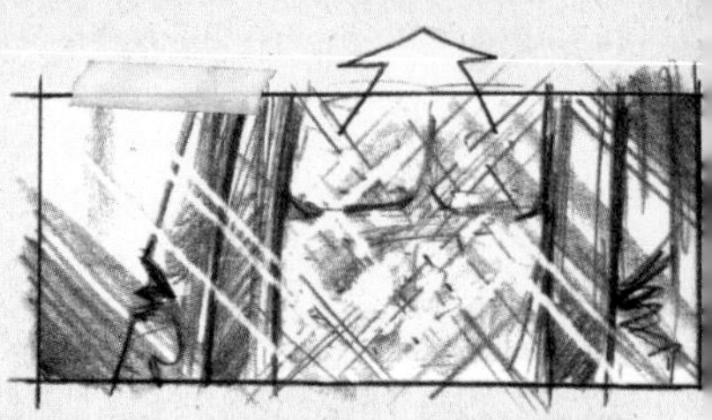

EDWARD IN THE SUNLIGHT WAS SHOCKING... His skin, white despite the faint flush from yesterday's hunting trip, literally sparkled, like thousands of tiny diamonds were embedded in the surface...A perfect statue, carved in some unknown stone, smooth like marble, glittering like crystal.

6:15 PM. Getting dark. Raining buckets. Line Producer Michele Imperato is tearing up, on the phone to L.A.: "We can't shoot the sun scene in the rain." We are packing up to leave when the rain stops. The clouds open up enough to make the sky brighten enough to shoot. We get 45 minutes to shoot the most pivotal scene. As Patrick says, "That's moviemaking." (It's his first film.)

The condors were used to reach into the forest and provide fill. The BeeBee light was brought up from L.A. to provide a strong direct beam on Edward.

← thanks, Stephenie! — That sounds EASY Not!

"DIAMONDS EMBEDDED IN THE SKIN" AND "SMOOTH LIKE MARBLE."
Diamonds sparkle because of the facets catching the light—but facets on Rob's face looked like a bad case of acne. SMOOTH didn't glitter and sparkle.

After months of tests, and several trips to I.L.M. (George Lucas' Industrial Light & Magic-Visual Effects company)—we created this look for Edward in the sun light. Rob's body was scanned (settle down girls) and mapped and various layers of effects were laid over it.

TO84
01:01:06:08
AT10:29:53:01
0099+07D
635584 7736+08A
R04:11:43:20
VT04:11:43:25.2
the tree root was cabled off to a high pic-point – then the SPECIAL FX man pulled it along with Rob – yanking it high into the air –
Later, the VFX team added flying dirt clods
As if you could fight me off

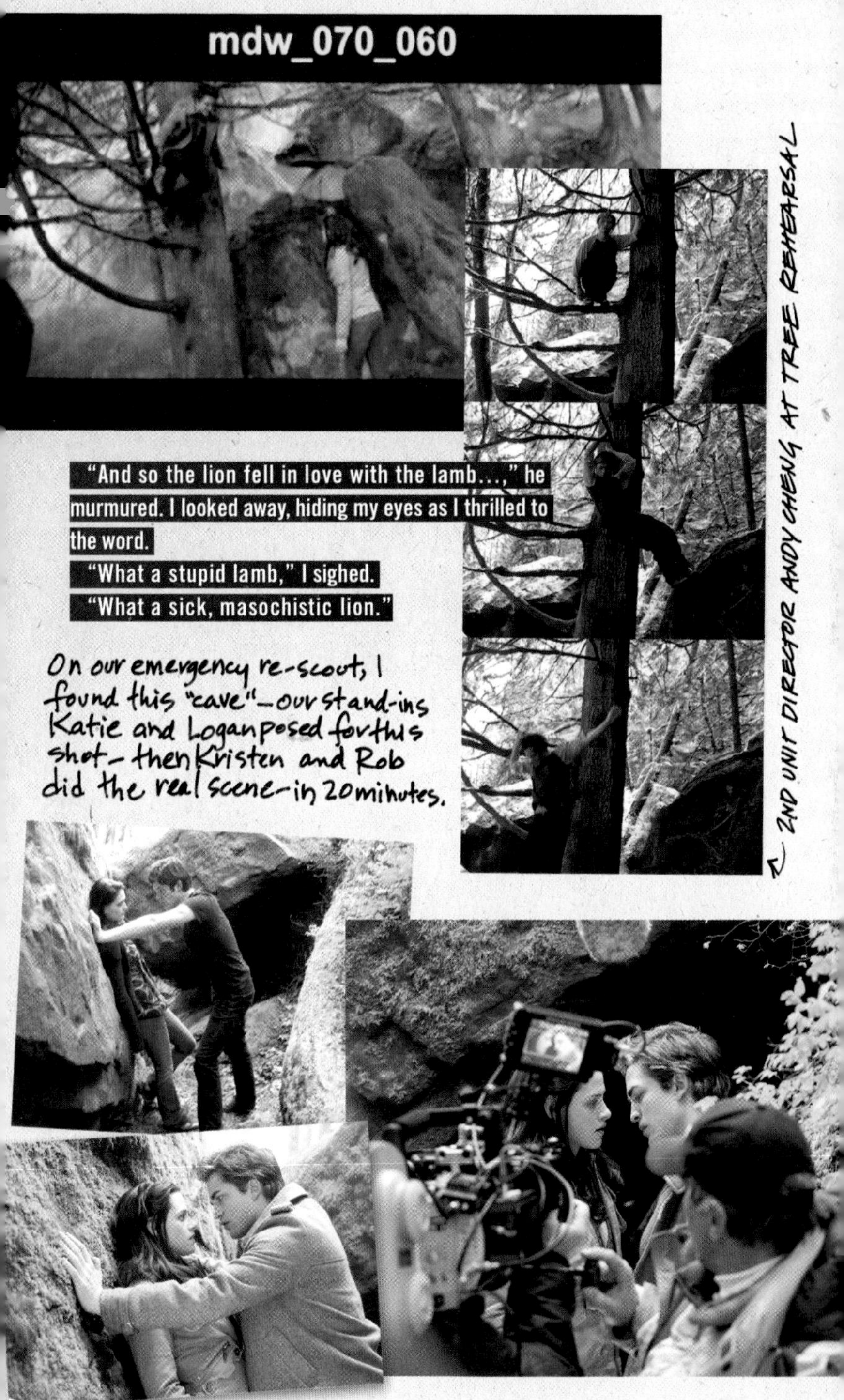
mdw_070_060
On our emergency re-scout, I found this "cave"—our stand-ins Katie and Logan posed for this shot—then Kristen and Rob did the real scene—in 20 minutes.
2ND UNIT DIRECTOR ANDY CHENG AT TREE REHEARSAL

"And so the lion fell in love with the lamb...," he murmured. I looked away, hiding my eyes as I thrilled to the word.

"What a stupid lamb," I sighed.

"What a sick, masochistic lion."

We never got to shoot a real "meadow" in Oregon. So in August, in Los Angeles, we shot this part of the scene.

BEFORE:
DRY FOREST

AFTER

Trying to re-connect with the intimate feeling we had when we shot the rest of the scene 4 months earlier.

Pretend like there's no one else around for 100 miles.

Right in the middle of the Griffith Park golf course is a Forest. Who knew?

Production Designer Steve Saklad brought in a sculpted carpet of lush grass and flowers, ferns and moss. We shot at the end of the day, at Magic Hour and added lots of fog -- to match Oregon.

Greetings, earthlings. I have come to take you to my planet!

Technocrane pullback to high wide shot

Note: I.L.M. later added the "sparkle FX" to Edward in this crane shot.

TREETOPS

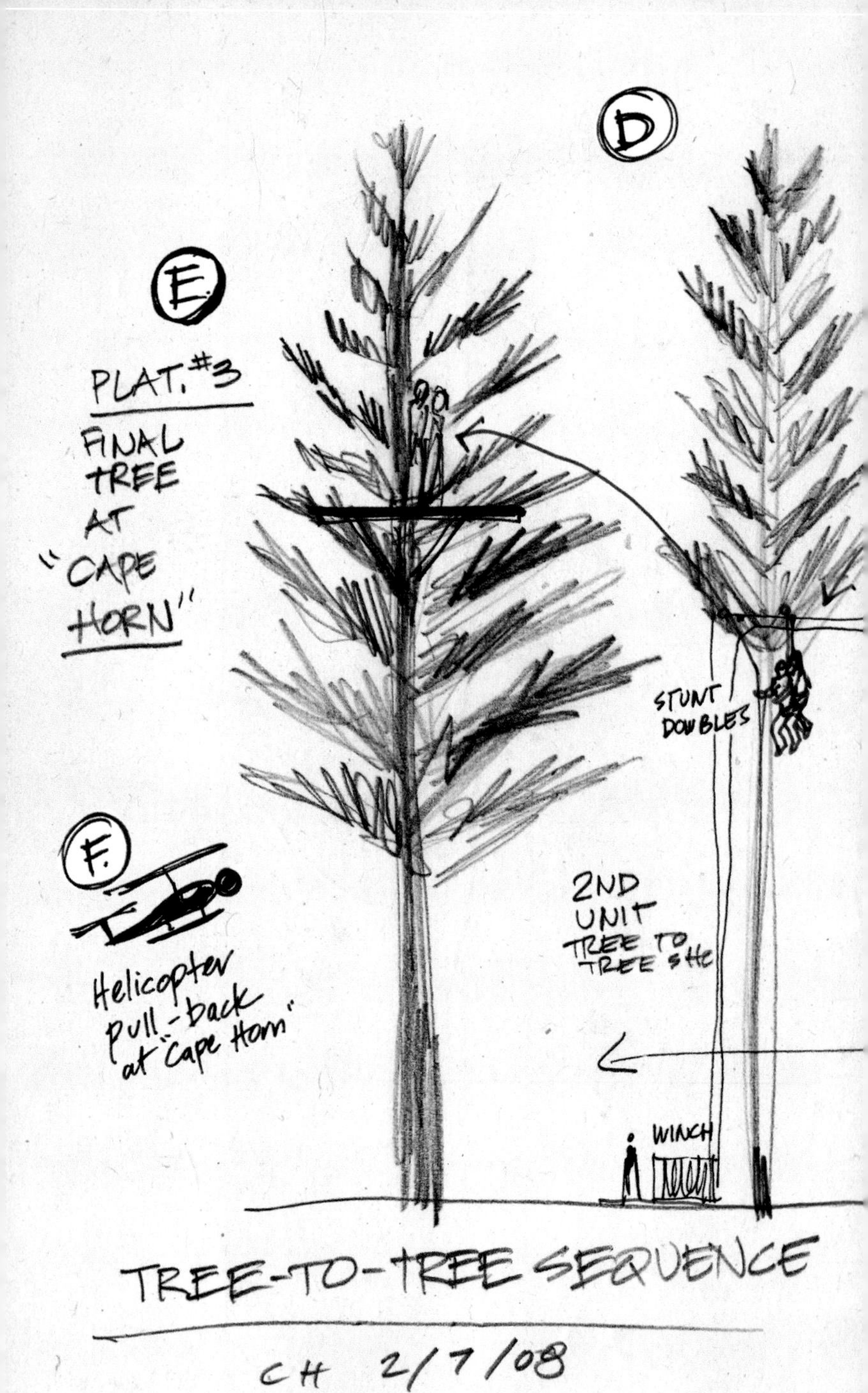
D
E
PLAT. #3
FINAL TREE AT "CAPE HORN"
STUNT DOUBLES
F.
Helicopter pull-back at "Cape Horn"
2ND UNIT TREE TO TREE SHC
WINCH
TREE-TO-TREE SEQUENCE
CH 2/7/08

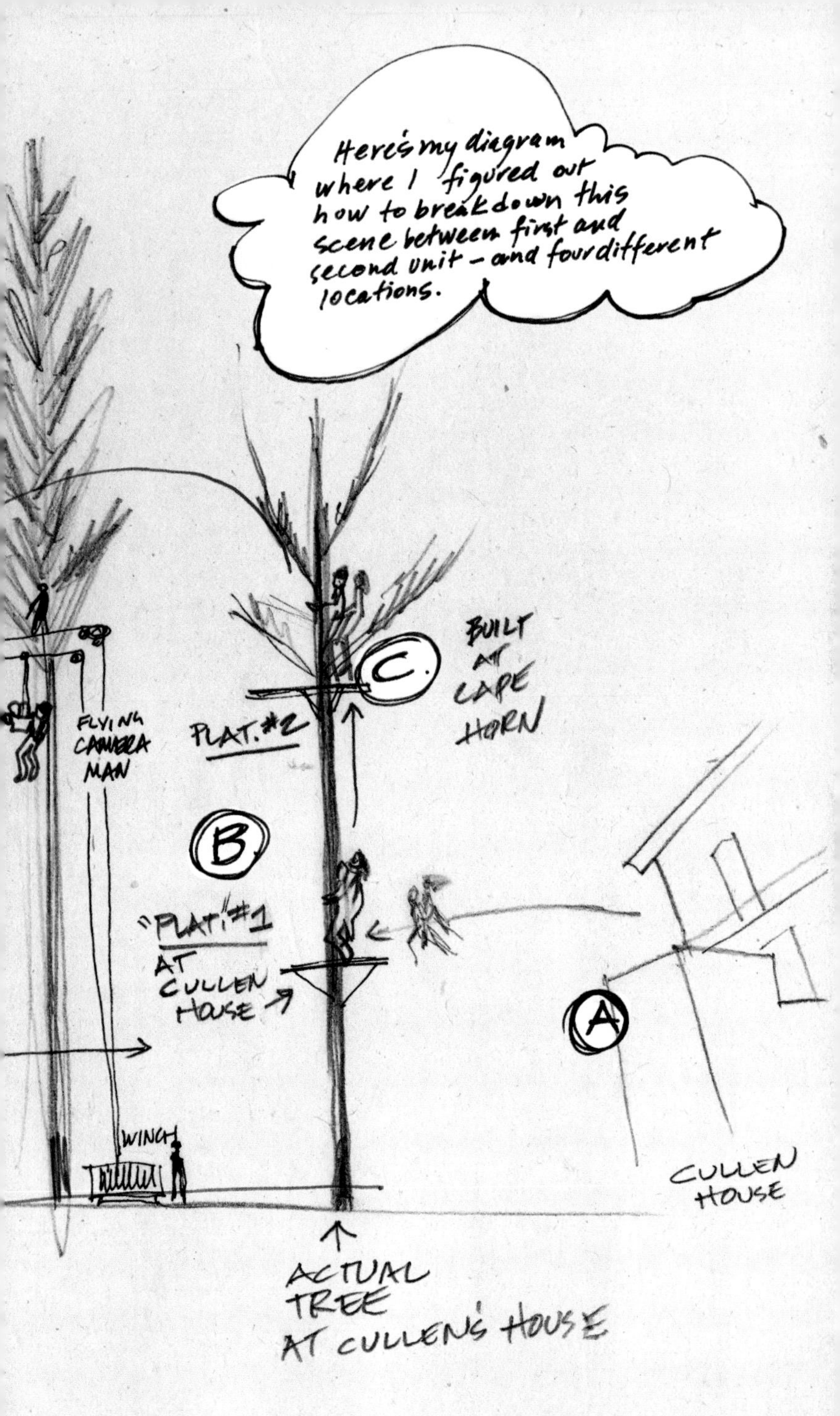

Here's my diagram where I figured out how to breakdown this scene between first and second unit – and four different locations.
FLYING CAMERA MAN
PLAT. #2
C.
BUILT AT CAPE HORN
B
"PLAT" #1 AT CULLEN HOUSE
A
WINCH
CULLEN HOUSE
ACTUAL TREE AT CULLEN'S HOUSE

I'm not afraid of you.

A.

CULLEN HOUSE

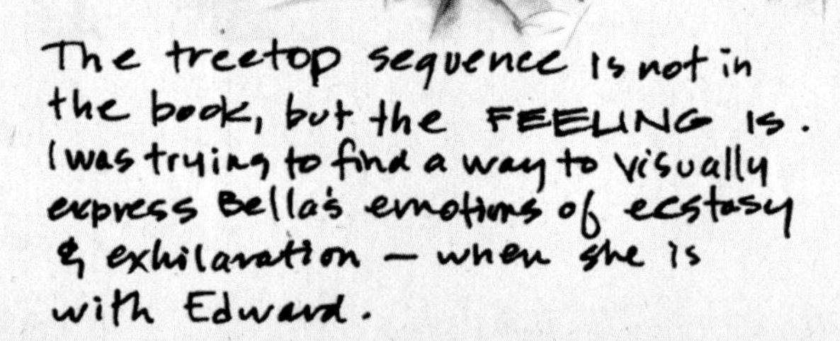

The treetop sequence is not in the book, but the FEELING is. I was trying to find a way to visually express Bella's emotions of ecstasy & exhilaration — when she is with Edward.

Stunt doubles wearing safety harnesses on a flying rig. One side rigged to a real tree on location — one side to a tower.

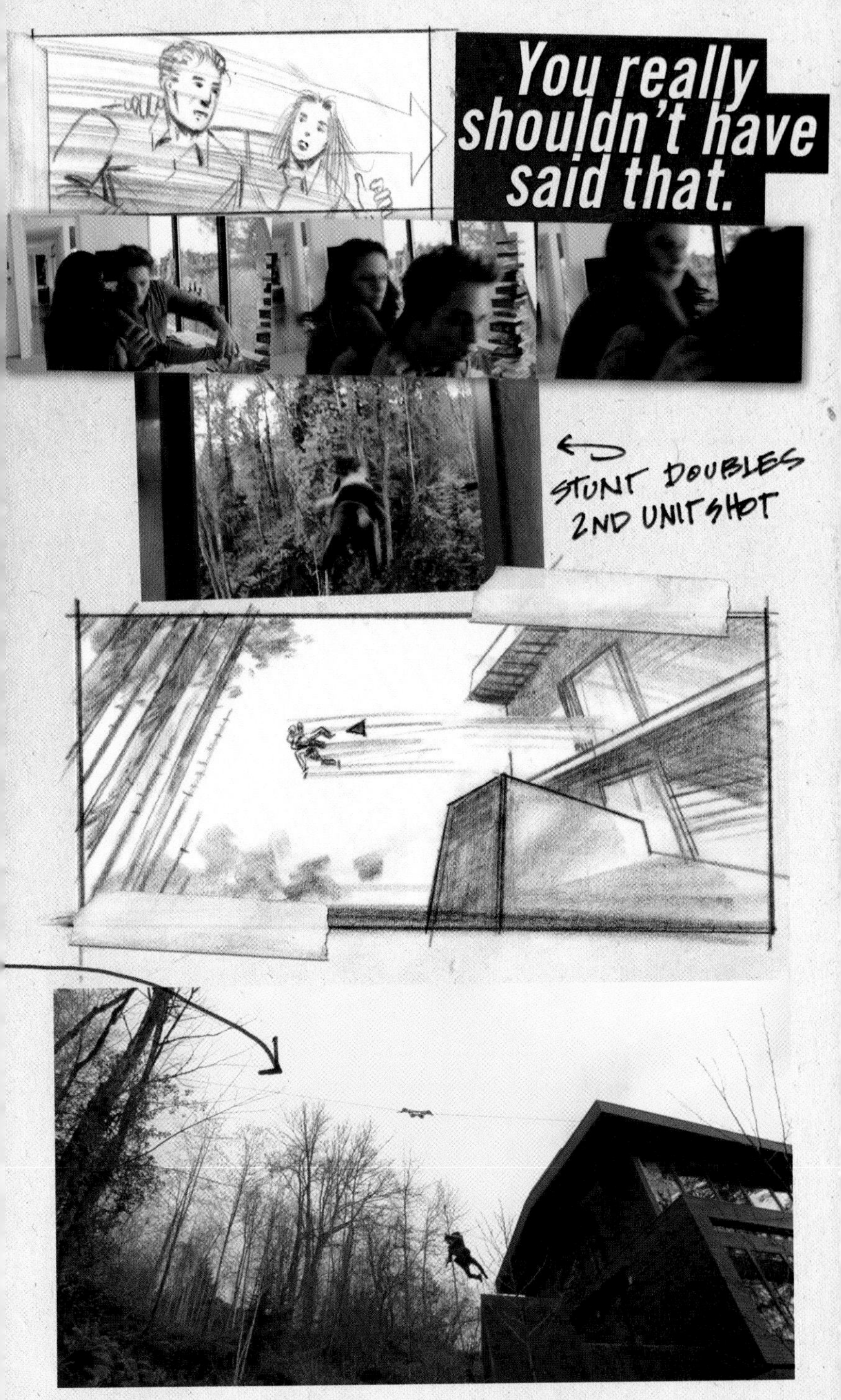
You really shouldn't have said that.
STUNT DOUBLES
2ND UNIT SHOT

B. Platform #2

Hold on tight, Spider Monkey!'

The nite before we shot this scene, I came up with 10 different lines and Rob chose the "spider monkey" line.

Stunt double Seth Duhame models the safety harness

Trust me?

C. Platform #3

D. 2ND UNIT — Andy Cheng shot all the cool treetop stunts at a remote location in Silver Springs, Oregon.

A TALE OF RIGGERS AND WINCHES

stunt doubles in tall trees

OUR 2ND AND LAST GREEN SCREEN SHOT IN THE FILM. 2ND UNIT SHOT THE BACKGROUND PLATES.

Key frame drawn by Philip Keller

All the storyboard artists were gone by this time...

DRIFTING PAST, THEY'RE INTOXICATED BY THE VIEW...

AND EACH OTHER...

E. PLATFORM #3

IS ON THE EDGE OF A CLIFF OVERLOOKING THE COLUMBIA RIVER GORGE.

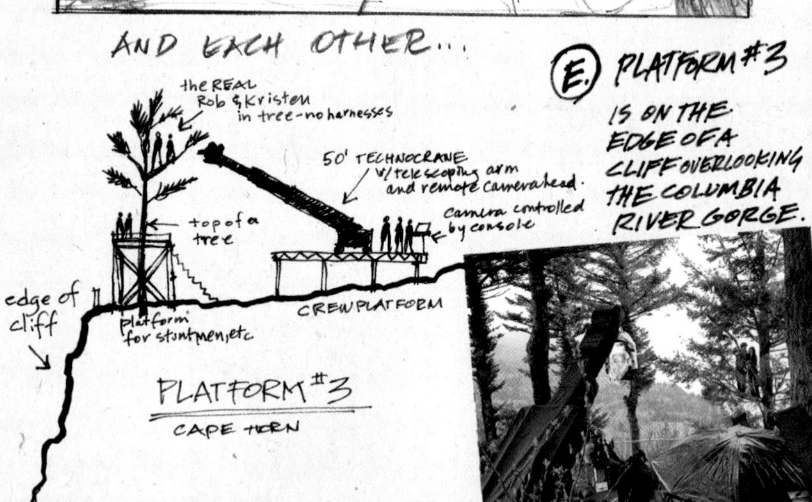

...so I drew these.

CAMERA MOVES UP THE TREE AS EDWARD HELPS BELLA CLIMB...

REVEALING THE STUNNING VIEW...

Note: wet stunt pads, heavy coats, & FEAR.

Yes, they were really in the trees!

Stunt doubles Paul and Helena free-climbed up this monster tree. Then they cabled off to the trunk to protect themselves against the powerful backwind from the helicopter rotor blades.

Andy supervised this final shot in the sequence from the helicopter using a Space Cam Huey mount. In the big sphere is a gyro-stabilized remotely controlled camera capable of shooting at virtually any camera angle. If you dont believe me, you can GOOGLE it. (I did.)

the
BASEBALL GAME

Early illustration by Marc Vena

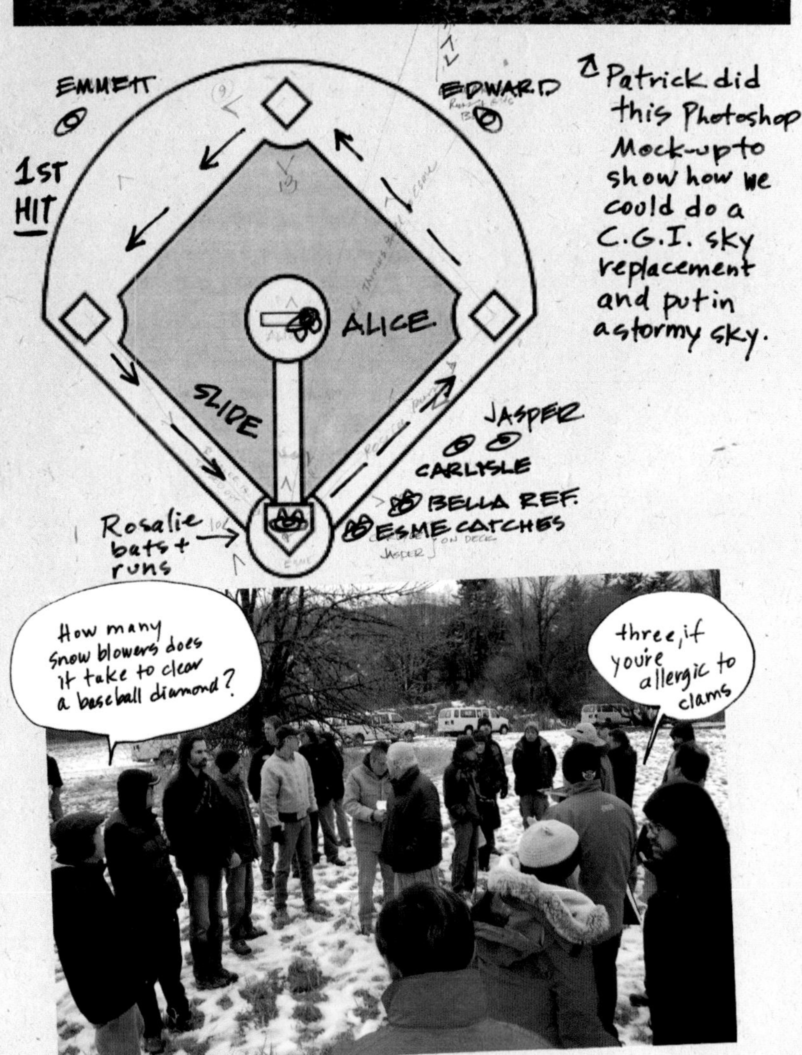
EMMETT
EDWARD
1ST HIT
ALICE
SLIDE
JASPER
CARLYSLE
BELLA REF.
ESME CATCHES
Rosalie bats + runs
↑ Patrick did this Photoshop Mock-up to show how we could do a C.G.I. sky replacement and put in a stormy sky.
How many snow blowers does it take to clear a baseball diamond?
three, if you're allergic to clams

All the department heads go to the tech scout to figure out baseball logistics.

we shot across the river from the falls.
MULTNOMAH
FALLS
COLUMBIA RIVER GORGE
NATIONAL SCENIC AREA

At one point, we thought we would film the baseball game at night. Then we added up the cost of the lights. Ouch.

1

NIGHT SKY OVER TREE LINE w/ LIGHTNING IN CLOUDS...

TILT-DOWN

...TO REVEAL BASEBALL FIELD IN CLEARING w/ CULLEN FAMILY & BELLA.

Steve Smith, Key Grip, constructed a "rain shelter" for close-ups.

Our first day at the baseball field was a torrential downpour. Not good for wigs or vampire make up.

Almost every sky had to be replaced in C.G.I. to get storm cloud consistency.
We got rained on the first day, and sun the next week, so when it finally got cloudy, we had 1½ days to shoot the entire sequence. YIKES.

Ashley rehearsing:
"It's time."

Ashley was struggling to learn to pitch until one day she watched a stunt girl and it just CLICKED.

Nikki worked hard with the baseball coach and became quite a SLUGGER.

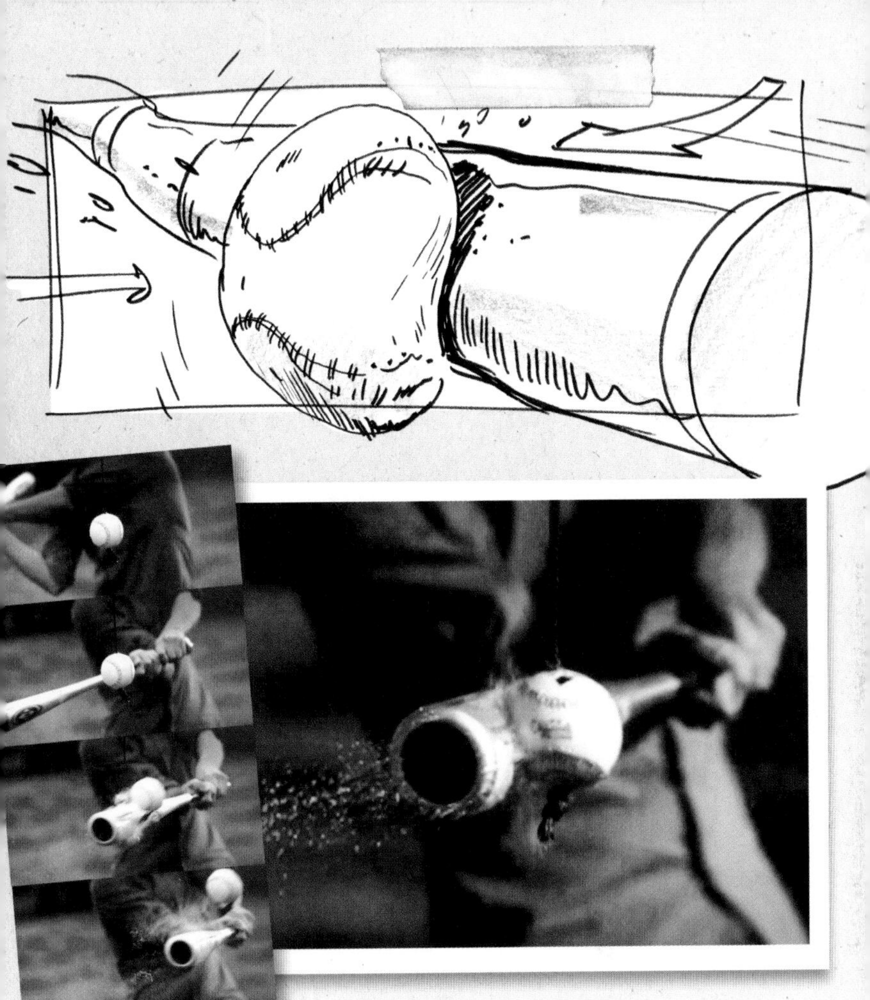

We did test shoots with a Hi-speed camera for vampire baseball hits.

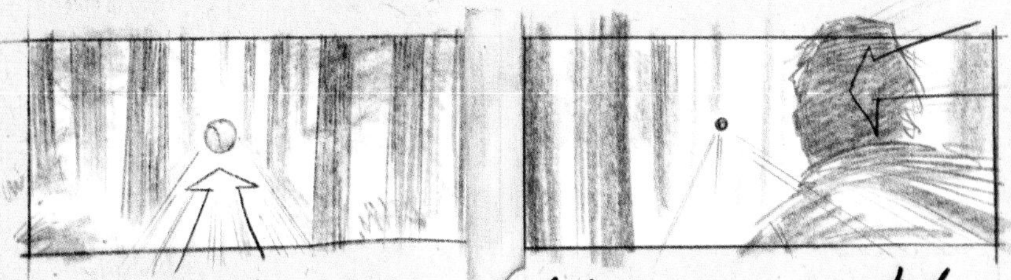

Rob Friedman - CEO of Summit, suggested this "Robin Hood" C.G.I. shot.

ROB AND HIS DOUBLE WERE PULLED BY CABLES ALONG A DOLLY TRACK FOR HI-SPEED RUNNING SHOTS
Here the camera and the stuntman are on the same computerized winch program so they will move at the same speed to keep the performer in the frame.

Peter suggested this "Babe Ruth" move in the rehearsal.
STUNT DOUBLES ON CABLE RIG SUSPENDED BETWEEN 2 TOWERS
SHOT CONTINUES
RIG IS REMOVED AND SKY IS REPLACED BY VFX
1
2ND UNIT
WIRE RIG REMOVAL
VFX SKY
POSSIBLE RAMP DOWN OR FREEZE IN MID-AIR
SHOT CONTINUES
ANGLE ADJUSTED SO WE LOSE E+E when we drop down to Dr. Culler
THE MID-AIR COLLISION

JACKSON NEEDS NO BASEBALL COACH— HE ALREADY HAD SKILZ.

At first I thought I'd have one of the chix go up the tree, but then when Kellan came on board – he kinda *had* to do the stunt →

2ND UNIT USED A GRADE-ALL (LIKE A GIANT FORKLIFT) TO DO THE WIRE RIGGING FOR THE TREE JUMP STUNT.

wires removed later 2
NiKKi hits the last ball and Alice gets a VISION:
They're moving so fast!

Hello, Folks ~ Welcome to Andy Cheng's

The cameramam, Patrick Loungway rides
the skateboard dolly - the actors walk on the magic carpet.

The magic carpet is like a moving sidewalk - leaves cover sheets of plexiglas which are pulled by the winch, An 8 men rigging crew makes it all happen - safely.

MAGIC CARPET RIDE...

the nomads appear out of the mist...

MAKE IT WORK, NOMADS. MAKE IT WORK.

Our first ideas of how the Nomads might look -- before they turned into the evil rockstar bloodsuckers that we know and love.

Richard Kidd, our VFX supervisor, had the actors catching clear plastic balls so they could be replaced later.

Dr. Cullen tries to keep things calm between the two clans.

"I'm the one with the wicked curve ball" came from a rehearsal improv.

YOU BROUGHT A SNACK?

(yes it's one of my favorite lines and I got to say it in all the auditions when I played James.)

the stand-off—
CLAN VS. CLAN.

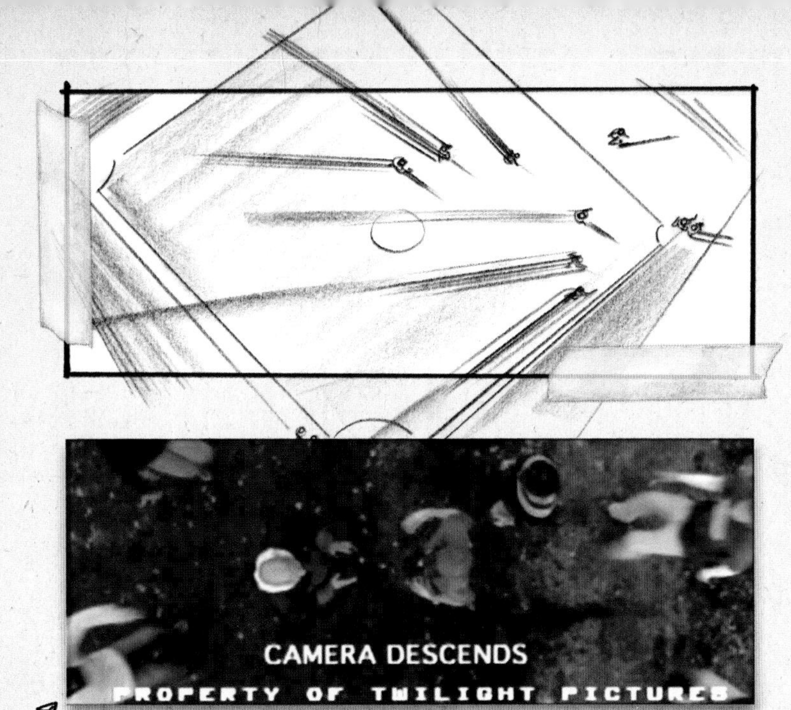

Rehearsal for overhead shot — done by 2ND UNIT

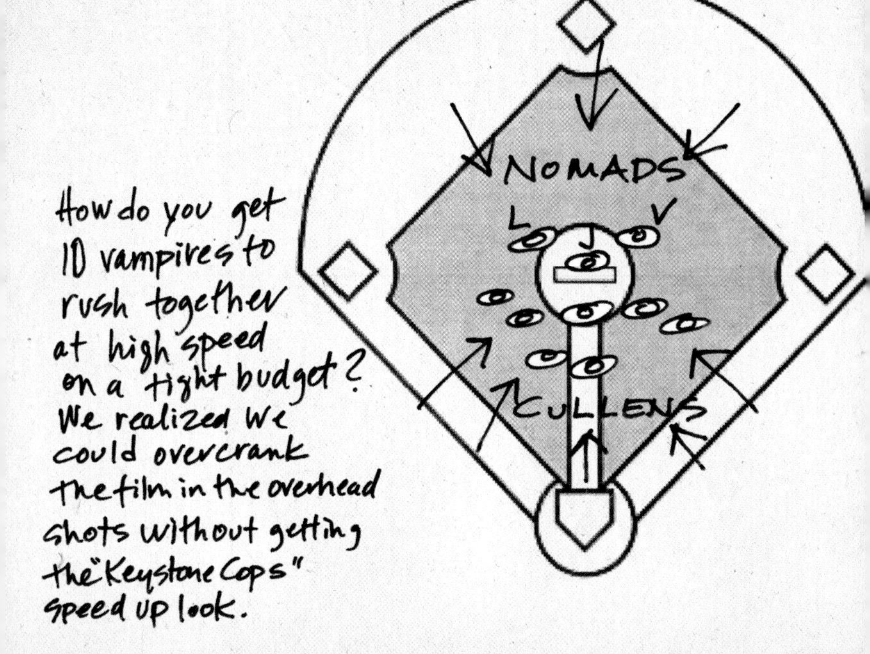

How do you get 10 vampires to rush together at high speed on a tight budget? We realized we could overcrank the film in the overhead shots without getting the "Keystone Cops" speed up look.

A TYPICAL DAY:

the crew is standing by. We've got 1/2 hour of daylight left – and 8 shots on my SHOT LIST. All 11 actors have just arrived in vans from base camp. We're finally ready to shoot. The magic words ring out: "ROLL CAMERA". But before I can say "action" –

Wait my wig is coming loose –
Sorry, gotta change the camera battery
Oops – I forgot my contacts.
I have to use the ladies room.
I think I'd be much more aggressive at this point.
Can we put our shoes on? I'm getting frostbite.
Elliot, we just lost a stop.
My handwarmer slipped down my pants – does it show?
Kristen has 10 minutes of skool left. We have to put her double in....
Katie's at base camp
the sky gradually darkens through the scene – then the chase scene is at nite – 2ND UNIT Did mad JEEPING through the woods

Early illustration by Marc Vena.

the BALLET STUDIO
HOW TO KILL A VAMPIRE

stunt rehearsals on stage ↙

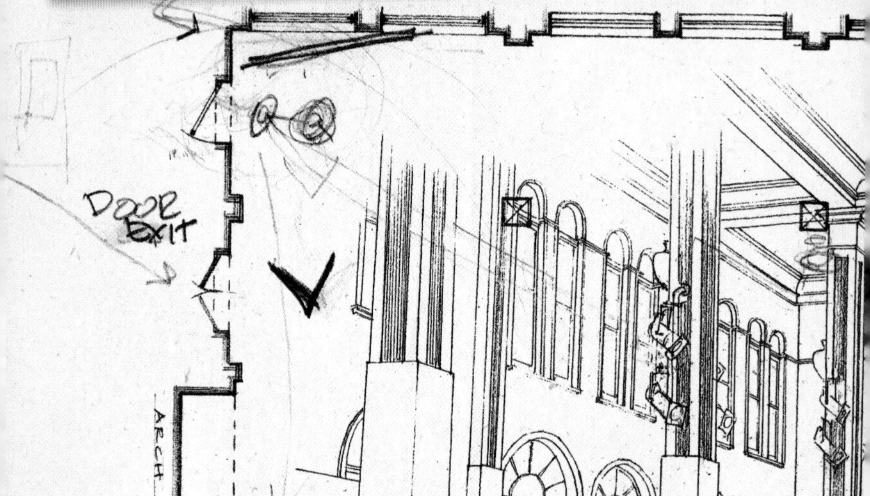

DOOR EXIT

ARCH

AM1 MASTER

JAMES FLINGS EDWARD

some of my early sketches

the ballet studio was constructed in a Portland warehouse. 60 pic points and 4 winches were built into the set by the stunt rigging crew.

5 THINGS TO REMEMBER WHEN YOU'RE SHOOTING IN A ROOM FULL OF MIRRORS:

1. DON'T DO IT. Everything is in the shot.
2. If you choose to do it anyway, watch *The Lady From Shanghai* and *Enter the Dragon*.
3. NOTE TO CREW: YOU CAN RUN, BUT YOU CAN'T HIDE.
4. If you see something bad in dailies, you can try to erase it in C.G.I. – if you have the bucks!
5. Dress for the set. Dave Galbraith, 1st Camera Assistant, models the All-Black Ninja look. I'm modeling a new idea: A MIRRORED CAPE. (NOTE: IT DIDN'T WORK.)

IN THIS STORYBOARD PANEL, YOU DON'T SEE BELLA'S FACE AND JAMES IS VERY SMALL IN THE FRAME, AND IT'S A STUNT. SO IT'S A 2ND UNIT SHOT.
IN THIS STORYBOARD PANEL, YOU SEE BELLA'S FACE, SO IT'S A FIRST UNIT SHOT.
CRACK!

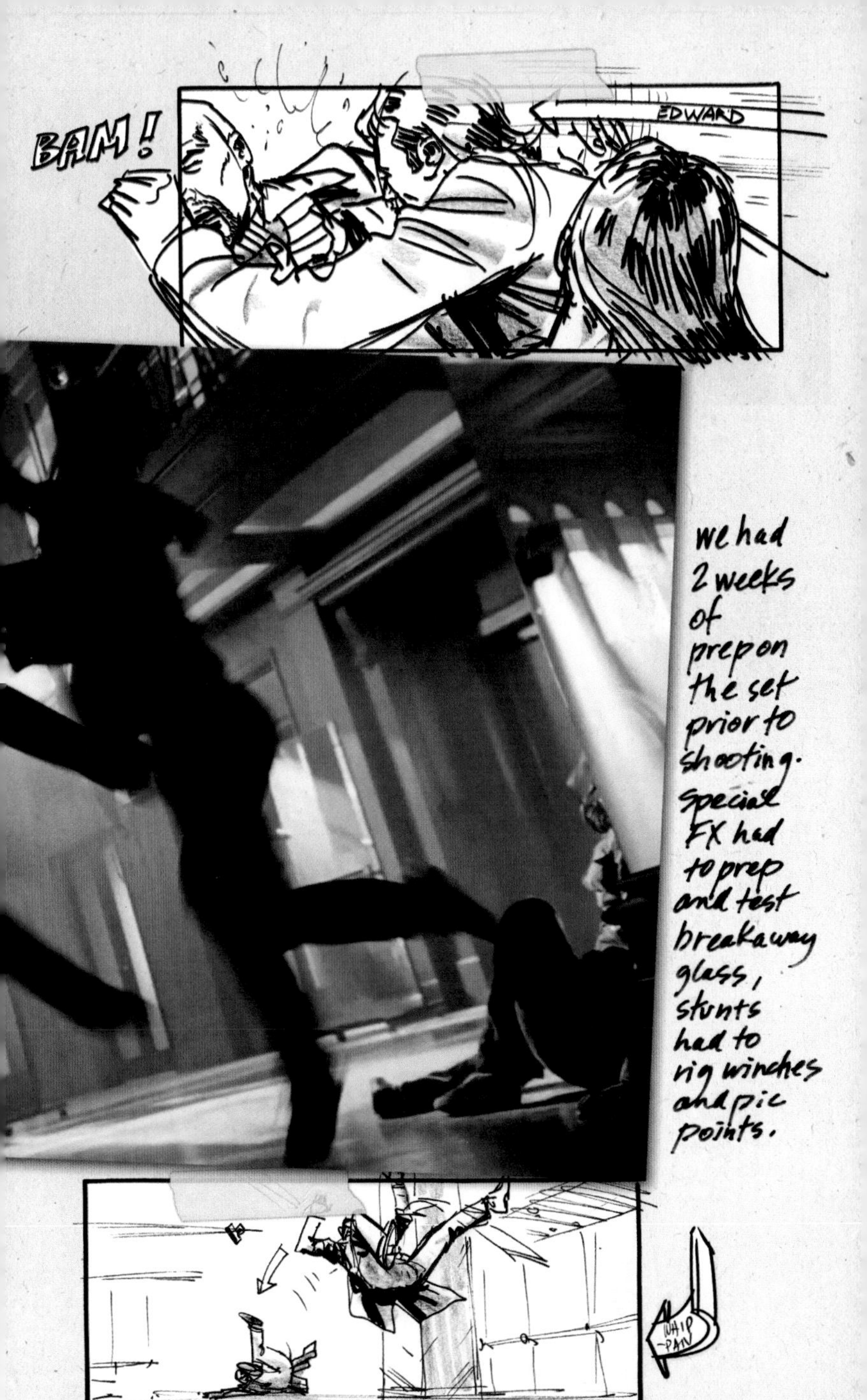

BAM!
EDWARD
we had 2 weeks of prep on the set prior to shooting. Special FX had to prep and test breakaway glass, stunts had to rig winches and pic points.
WHIP-PAN

First and Second UNIT SHOTS HAVE TO BE CAREFULLY PLANNED so that they will match when cut together.

7years of GOOD LUCK?
we tested 6 types of Breakaway Mirror Glass—different thicknesses, paper-backed, tempered, etc. For this scene, James smashes Edward into candy glass.
I had to arrange all the broken bits on the James double because we shot the "aftermath" before we shot the stunt.

The actors rehearse with the stunt department behind the ballet studio set. We shot this scene first, completely out of chronological order, so it was challenging for the actors both emotionally (in terms of character arc development) and physically (coordinating with stunt doubles and breakaway mirrors.)

ALL HAIL TO 2ND UNIT!
Director Andy Cheng and cinematographer Patrick Loongway matched Elliot's lighting exactly. They shot on weekends after we finished all the first unit shots.
CRASH!
Paul was on a flying rig when he crashed into the window.

INSERT YOUR FAVORITE
EDWARD FOTO HERE

The fight is not really described in the book because Bella is unconscious from the venom. So Andy and I brainstormed ideas that would follow Stephenie's rules. We thought that these two vampires would be trying to rip each other apart—not hitting each other because that wouldn't hurt. I felt that when James bit Bella, Edward would be so enraged that he would resort to his "animal" nature and make the lunge—plowing James into the floor.

Early illustration by Marc Vena.

DIVE BOMB!

We built the set 18" off the ground to create a channel for the dolly track. The actors & stuntmen were pulled along on a "skateboard" dolly.

yes, the stunt guys earned their pay on this one!

Breakaway balsa floorboards

After we saw the dailies, I had VFX add some boards flying directly at the camera. POW!

Early illustration by Marc Vena.

"TWILIGHT" "Ballet Studio no. 1"

Marc Vena 2007

C/U of Edward & James plowing thru last bit of the floor into BREAKAWAY
mn and BREAKAWAY MIRROR. (or whatever piece is possible/safe) (time
nitting)
TWO SHOT at column Edward lifts James up
1st UNIT - NO BELLA
CAM
CAM
Bella is
Edward throws James
olumn – end with James slumped to ground.
MATCH
MY SHOT LISTS ARE COLOR-CODED. BLUE IS FOR SHOTS WITHOUT KRISTEN. SINCE SHE WAS A MINOR FOR 3/4 OF THE SHOW, WE COULD ONLY SHOOT WITH HER FOR 5½ HRS
G2- G9 OMIT
oking toward arch)Edward
They try to bite each
G10. TWO SHOT – PROFILE
PRE-BROKEN REPLACEMENT PLASTER
JAMES
G14. OTS Edward as he bites James an
G15. SHOT of Edward rips off a piece of
SWISH PAN over
G11/12 Bella screams.... SWISH PAN over
starting to bite James.
G16. Close on Bella shocked.. reacting to
(flip the storyboard)
G13 Over Bella onto Edward as he bites James.
START 8:15 - 6:45 Bella gone
G17 OMIT
then becomes
Rob and Cam wanted to go "off book" and do this part of the fight "freestyle" - unchoreographed - FIERCE...
H6. (Pick up from
rushes to her.. Alic
TIGHTER THREE SHOT on siblings
H5a. TIGHTER THREE SHOT on siblings (Photo storyboard)
B CAM?
three shot or over Bella.
three Cullen siblings jumping off balcony and run toward
2nd UNIT
... so Elliot grabbed the camera and just flowed with the actors - hand-held "thirteen" style.

Make up Man
Rolf Keppler
shows his scar skillz

It was late at night when we filmed the final ferocious bite — we realized we didn't have any "skin." So we hit up the craft service table, as shown below

D.I.Y. MAKE UP F/X

Put on sanitary gloves, or wash hands thoroughly. Remove cheese from packaging. Discard packaging.

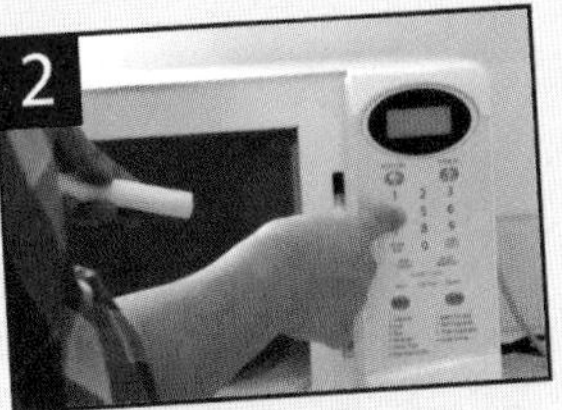

Place cheese on microwave safe dish, place dish in oven, close door, press **START**.

Microwave on **LOW** for **45** seconds or until cheese becomes rubbery. Cooking times may vary.

Cheese will be **VERY HOT**. Allow "skin" to cool to room temperature. Clean desired area, then apply. **ENJOY!**

By this point in the fight scene, I felt that Edward has moved even deeper into his violent animal nature—he is further and further from his sympathetic, human self as he viciously bites James. This is the moment that Carlisle steps in to remind Edward of his true nature. Edward stops his attack, reconnects with his heart, and goes to save Bella.

original concept with skylight dome—before I learned that the ceiling would have to be rigged with tracks and pic points →

the cavalry arrives:
Kellan, Ashley, and Jackson got to harness up and fly.

BURN the PIECES

the propane-fueled fire was built on a triangular metal base with 3 flame bars. We could only burn it for 45 seconds due to heat build up.

EDWARD SUCKS VENOM FROM BELLA'S HAND

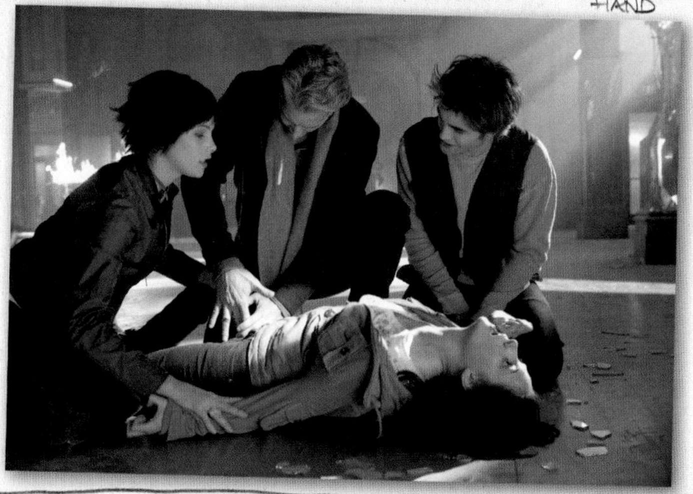

WARNING TO ASPIRING FILMMAKERS:

The storyboard artists were long gone, so I drew these

MY FAVORITE IDEA: ALICE TWISTS OFF JAMES' HEAD.

Grrl power!

FIRE WAS SUPERVISED BY PROFESSIONALS. CEILING PIECES WERE REMOVED AND A FIRE MARSHALL WAS PRESENT FOR SAFETY.

the venom travels up her arm... into her bloodstream

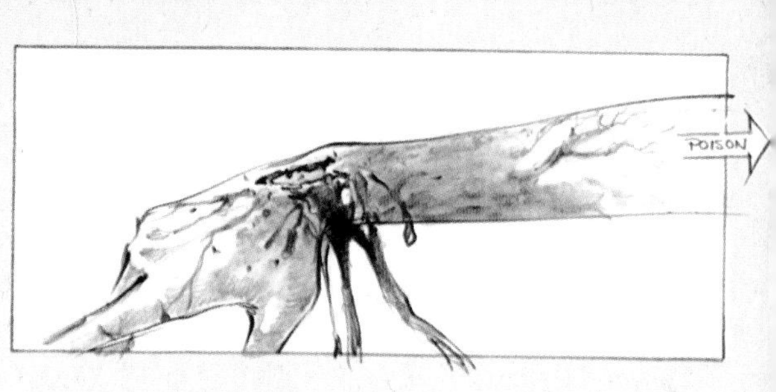

When we were filming this scene where Edward is saving Bella's life—draining the venom from her veins—Kristen and I looked at each other: I think we realized at the same time just how emotionally profound this moment was for Bella.

DEATH
is
PEACEFUL,
EASY.
I wanted to film an underwater dream sequence for Bella's "death" but it was nixed for budgetary reasons. So I worked with P.I.C., our title design company, to create a dream sequence out of scenes we had already shot... almost like Bella saw her life flashing before her.
TILT
TILT
PULL
PULL

Music

the soundtrack

Rob's 2 songs:

Kristen & Nikki kept telling me about Rob's songs and his voice – but he would never let me hear him sing. "I'll bring you a CD tomorrow" turned into 2 months. Finally I convinced him to go into my friend Karl Leiker's studio in his Venice apartment and just lay something down.

He sat in a low Japanese chair in a tiny room and sang and played guitar – all on the same track ... 6 songs...

Rob's songs were raw and emotional. Adam Smalley, our music editor, tried the songs against picture. "Never Think" fit in beautifully with the restaurant scene, but "Let Me Sign" made Bella's death scene in the Ballet Studio much more powerful. Even Rob agreed, so he went into Bright Street Studios and recorded the songs with a cellist – and Adam, Karl, and Kenny Woods at the boards.

One of my favorite days was watching Rob record. He sang the songs dozens of times, but no two takes were alike. The music seemed to flow from somewhere deep inside.

How we picked songs for the SOUNDTRACK

Haley visits the edit room.

Paramore

1. We started with Stephenie's playlist. Muse, Radiohead, Linkin Park and Collective Soul – all came from there.

2. Alex Patsavas – music supervisor – sends tons of music to the editing room.

3. Nancy Richardson – editor – cuts scenes with songs in them, finding out what works. Some of her first choices, like the Black Ghosts song at the opening, made it to the final movie.

4. Back in L.A. – Nancy, me and Adam Smalley, our music editor, all work madly to figure out the perfect songs for the emotions of each scene. For example, you can't have strong lyrics cutting through important dialogue.

THE TWILIGHT SONG – PARAMORE ♡ Hey!

HOW CAN I DECIDE WHAT'S RIGHT WHEN YOU'RE CLOUDING UP MY MIND. I CANT WIN YOUR LOSING FIGHT ALL THE TIME.
NOW CAN I EVER OWN WHATS MINE WHEN YOU'RE ALWAYS TAKING SIDES. BUT YOU WONT TAKE AWAY MY PRIDE NO NOT THIS TIME

CHORUS → HOW DID WE GET HERE? I USED TO KNOW YOU SO WELL
HOW DID WE GET HERE? I THINK I KNOW

THE TRUTH IS HIDING IN YOUR ~~EYES~~ EYES AND ITS HANGIN ON YOUR TONGUE, JUST BOILING IN MY BLOOD BUT YOU THINK THAT I CANT SEE WHAT KIND OF MAN THAT YOU ARE. IF YOU'RE A MAN AT ALL. WELL, I WILL FIGURE THIS ONE OUT ON MY OWN.

→ IM SCREAMING I LOVE YOU SO
→ BUT MY THOUGHTS YOU CANT DECODE

CHORUS: HOW DID WE GET HERE... (CHORUS)

DO YOU SEE WHAT WE'VE DONE? WE'VE GONE AND MADE SUCH FOOLS OF OURSELVES.

CHORUS → HOW DID WE GET HERE! I USED TO KNOW YOU SO WELL
HOW DID WE GET HERE? I THINK I KNOW

THERE IS SOMETHING I SEE IN YOU
IT MIGHT KILL ME
BUT I WANT IT TO BE TRUE

← Haley's lyrics for "Decode"

5. Alex scores a record deal with Atlantic. Haley from Paramore, Mute Math, and Perry Farrell visit the edit room and do special re-mixes of their songs.

6. At the last second, it comes together into our album.

Alex Patsavas ⟶

Perry Farrell and Etty Lau Farrell

Mute Math

the Score

notes from my first phone call with the composer ↗

CARTER BURWELL

Vampirism metaphor – a way of describing adolescence so well

what will it look like.

SPEED – MOVING FAST – cool slow moment life span... time ①

↳ SOUND COMES WITH THEM

slo...... speed..... RATCHET UP IN SPEED

10 x faster – UNIQUE.

Right sketches fast – synth sketches melodies...

Suite of Music – its own music world

struggle for intimacy – over obstacles

way it's recorded – suggesting extreme closeness

(instrument – electronic – so close 1" away from the mike – NOT A reverberative space...

uncomfortable sense

LONDON CALLING

Adam Smalley (music editor) and I met Carter in LONDON for the recording of the score.

I've made several trips to the junkyard to get some bits 'n bobs for this – for Carter. I had a large cowbell made.

predator

B.F.G.
Big Fat Gorgon.

speed

crunchy
not to syncopated

want to add some metal?

Carter Burwell conducts the London musicians at AIR LYNDHURST studios – founded by "the fifth Beatle" – Sir George Martin – inside a church built in the 1880's. Radiohead and other amazing bands have recorded here....

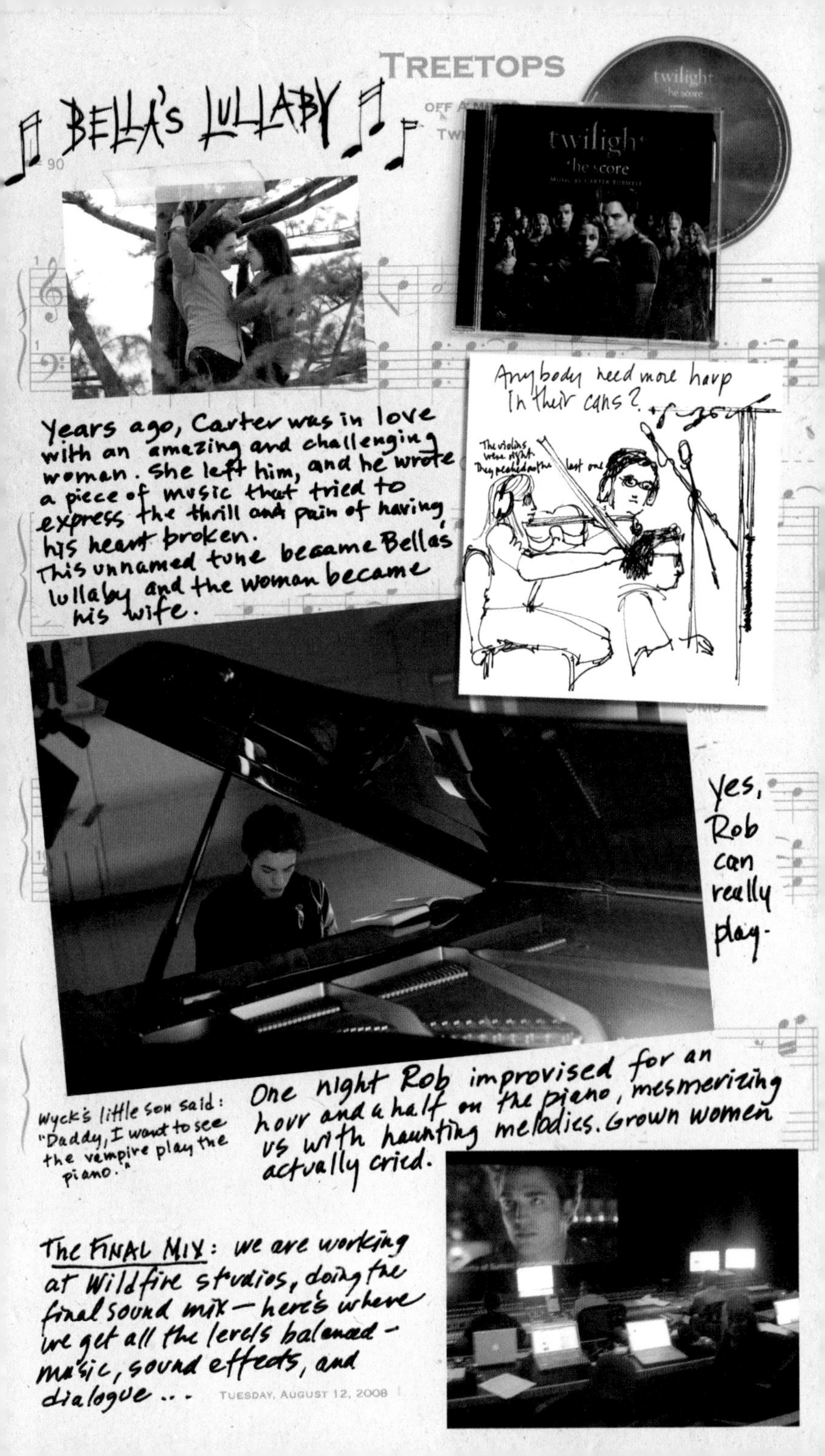

TREETOPS
BELLA'S LULLABY
twilight
the score
Anybody need more harp
In their cans?
The violins
were right.
They peaked on the last one
Years ago, Carter was in love with an amazing and challenging woman. She left him, and he wrote a piece of music that tried to express the thrill and pain of having his heart broken.
This unnamed tune became Bella's lullaby and the woman became his wife.
Yes, Rob can really play.
Wyck's little son said: "Daddy, I want to see the vampire play the piano."
One night Rob improvised for an hour and a half on the piano, mesmerizing us with haunting melodies. Grown women actually cried.
The FINAL MIX: we are working at Wildfire studios, doing the final sound mix — here's where we get all the levels balanced — music, sound effects, and dialogue . . .
TUESDAY, AUGUST 12, 2008

VISUAL FX

the DEER CHASE

stunt double jumps on to stunt pad at silver springs

+

real deer jumps over log at Silver Springs (grown men chased it over)

=

Richard Kidd, our Visual Effects supervisor composited the two shots together.

A 3-D Deer model was built to add "wiggle" to the deer's rear at the end of the shot.

VIRTUAL FOREST

RICHARD KIDD'S company, Catalyst Media, created the virtual forest environment to perform a 3-D composite with volumetric light beams, the real deer, the 3-D deer, and the stuntman plates.

Early design by Dereck Sonnenburg.
Composite supervision by Wolf Machin.

SOME IDEAS JUST DON'T WORK

THIS IS ONE OF THEM.

DEER HEAD

MOUNTED TO A MOUNTAIN BIKE FLYING OVER A RAMP.

... SOUNDED GOOD ON PAPER.

Nancy Richardson, the editor, and I found that we needed an establishing shot of the school for the rainy day scene.

BEFORE

AFTER

LIGHTNING, STORM CLOUDS & RAIN ADDED

WE TOOK A "FRAME GRAB" OFF THE AVID AND I WROTE NOTES—THEN PETRA HOLTORF-STRATTON, OUR VFX PRODUCER, FINDS MONEY IN OUR BUDGET TO SQUEEZE IN "ONE MORE SHOT."

SKY REPLACEMENT
•ADD STORMCLOUDS
•ADD LIGHTNING
•REMOVE CABLES

AFTER

Spot the Differences

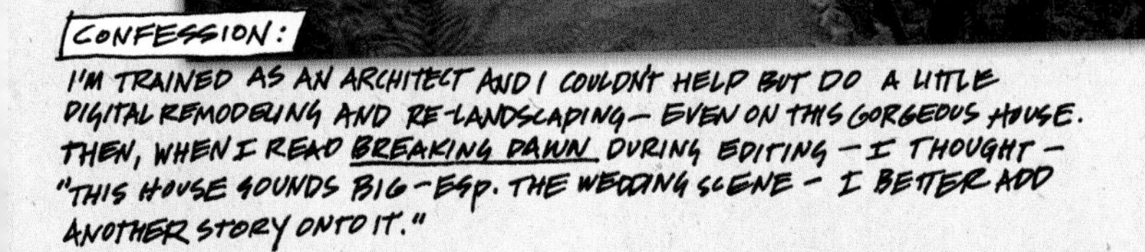

CONFESSION:
I'M TRAINED AS AN ARCHITECT AND I COULDN'T HELP BUT DO A LITTLE DIGITAL REMODELING AND RE-LANDSCAPING—EVEN ON THIS GORGEOUS HOUSE. THEN, WHEN I READ BREAKING DAWN DURING EDITING—I THOUGHT—"THIS HOUSE SOUNDS BIG—ESP. THE WEDDING SCENE—I BETTER ADD ANOTHER STORY ONTO IT."

Our water truck had a slight mishap on the way to set...*
* the driver walked away

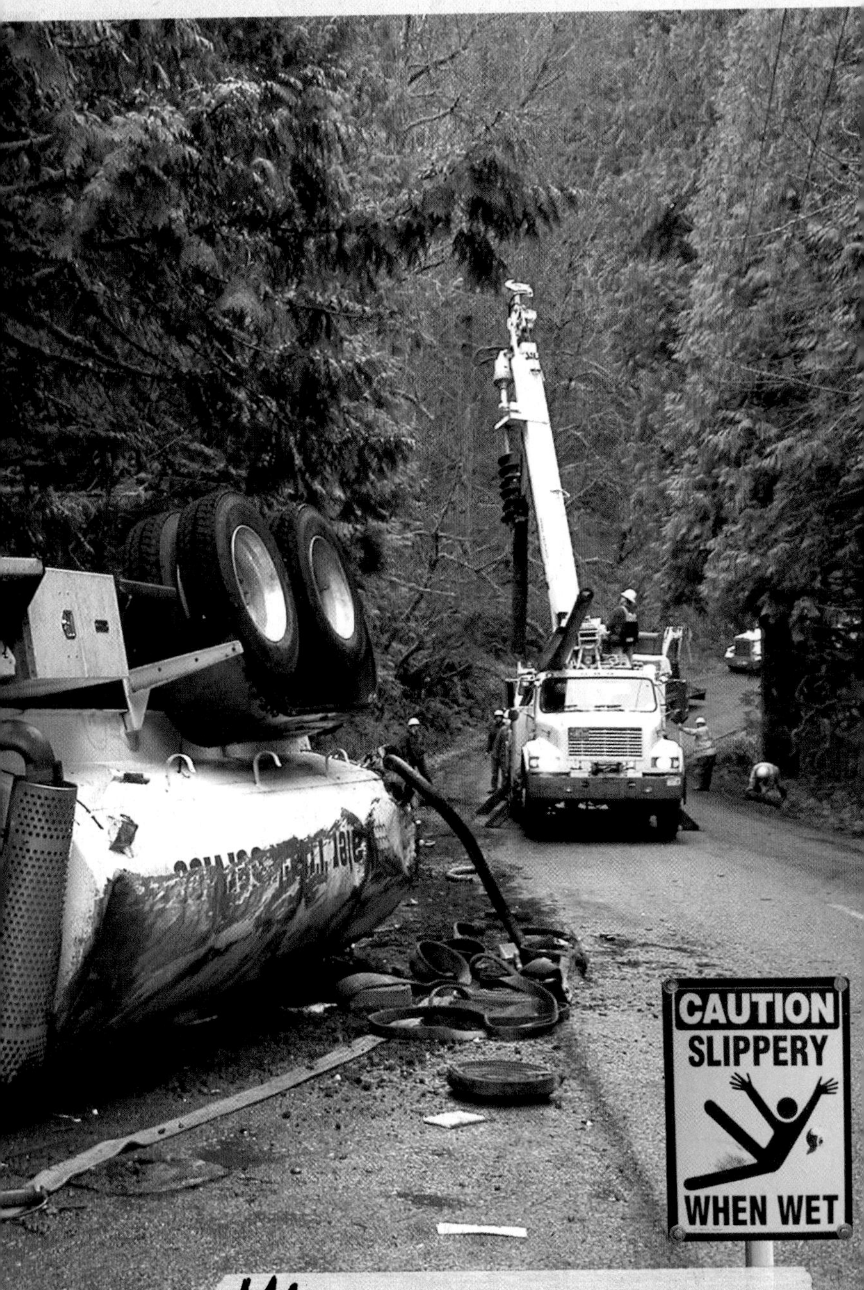
CAUTION
SLIPPERY
WHEN WET

Misery, meet disaster...

1ST PLACE WORST DAY

EVERYTHING HAD TO BE WRAPPED IN PLASTIC — BUT STILL 2 STEADICAM MONITORS WERE RUINED. THE CAMERA CREW WENT TO A HOTEL THAT NITE AND DRIED OUT ALL THE EQUIPMENT TIL 4AM.

CREW HAND-CARRIED EQUIPMENT 1 MILE ACROSS SLIPPERY ROCKS. THEY WERE NOT HAPPY.

HORIZONTAL DRIVING RAIN
this scene WAS supposed to be around a campfire on the beach - but no one would shoot there anymore, so we had to move it to dryer land.
FREEZING TEMPERATURES
I thought if we moved the scenes into the surfer van, at least the girls could wrap up in blankets and stay warm. So I ran through the parking lot asking other surfers if I could use their vans for a windblock.
CAN U SAY: X-TREME WEATHER
the actors are freezing, the crew is threatening to walk, and the lunch tent just blew over, Wyck.
Keep shooting.

PRODUCTION SUPERVISOR CRAIG CANNOLD & PRODUCER WYCK GODFREY.

Sammy stands in for Edward on the tech scout a week before shooting.

Don't worry, there won't be snow in April...

VR VT082
AT 05:32:15:28
??639797 8455+04
CASINO MONTE-CARLO
TYPICAL PHONE CALL:
FROM MICHAEL VIGLIETTA, 2ND UNIT FIRST A.D.:
"I'm trying to get that exterior shot of the prom for you, but we couldn't get the Volvo and it's snowing heavily."
Frequently, the sky would darken and it would suddenly
HAIL
22°F
EVEN THE FROGS WERE COLD
Look at the size of the coats Rob, Kristen, and the crew are wearing.

Through rain, sleet, and snow, we got it done and the movie went out into the world...
Twilight
(probably your biggest fan)
a fan
I would be more then happy

the best book she had
her twilight
Taylor has
Body Karate
going on!!!
"GO Taylor"
twilight
WESTWOOD
Mania
Crepúsculo
El Best-Seller mundial
muy pronto cobrará vida
Twilight was the best movie I've
seen in all my life. I loved the thrill I

thanks to...

BOOK DESIGN TEAM
Susan Burig
David Caplan
Zach Fannin
Ben Hardwicke
Catherine Hardwicke
Jamie Marshall
Nikki Ramey
Amanda Rosa
Patrick Smith
Megan Tingley

BOOK CONTRIBUTORS
Gilles Bensimon
Dan Bishop
Carter Burwell
Andy Cheng
Wendy Chuck
Elliot Davis
Shepherd Frankel
Trevor Goring
Philip Keller
Richard Kidd
Bruce Lawson
Patrick Loungway
James Lin
Beth Melnick
Oksana Nedavniaya
Deana Newcomb
Cynthia Nibler
Irene Hardwicke Olivieri
Alex Patsavas
Ian Phillips
Chris Ryan
Erin Schneider
Gene Serdena
Kathy Shorkey
Peter Sorel
PIC Agency
The Twilight Art Department
Jeanne Van Phue
Marc Vena
Deverill Weekes
Venice Paparazzi

VERY SPECIAL THANKS TO
Stephenie Meyer
Kristen Stewart
Robert Pattinson

BIG THANKS TO TEAM SUMMIT
Rob Friedman
Patrick Wachsberger
Bob Hayward
Erik Feig
Nancy Kirkpatrick
Vivian Mayer
Andi Isaacs
Amy Tillman
Geoff Shaevitz
Gillian Bohrer

THANKS TO
Melissa Rosenberg
Karen Rosenfelt
Greg Mooradian
Wyck Godfrey
Mark Morgan
Ken Kaplan
Stephanie Ritz
Nick Frenkel
Rowena Arguelles
Bebe Lerner
John Peed & Nicole Dietrichs - Cold Open
Chris Cook - *Forks Forum* - Newspaper (www.forksforum.com)
Lori Kelso - Forks Coffee Shop
Kevin Rupprecht - Forks High School
Diane Schostak - Olympic Peninsula Visitor Bureau
Tim Tasker - TGT Stickers
Editors Guild Magazine
Julie Jackson - Jackson Shrub

WAIT! THERE'S MORE... As I'm finishing these notes, I keep remembering so many other people that helped make the film—each contributing in their own unique way. Check out the CAST and CREW credits—all these people WORKED HARD.

But it's the incredible fans that encouraged us the whole time!

Love to all,
Catherine

ART BY KATHY SHORKEY: P. 22 mid painting, bot lt painting, P. 26 mid painting, P. 26 mid watercolor, P. 30 all watercolors, P. 32 bot mid painting P. 40 mid watercolor, P. 41 mid watercolor **ART BY WENDY CHUCK:** P. 24 bot series of photos, P. 25 bot series of photos, P. 29 bot series of photos, P. 31 bot series of photos, P. 33 bot series of photos, P. 34 bot series of photos, P. 35 bot series of photos, bot rt sketch, P. 36 bot series of photos, P. 40-41 bot series of photos. **ART BY OKSANA NEDAVNIAYA:** P. 24-25 center sketch, P. 27 center sketch, P. 28 - 29 center sketch, P. 31- 39 center sketch, **ART BY PETER SOREL:** P. ii-iii centerfold photo, P. 11 mid lt photo, P. 24 mid lt, P. 25 top rt, P. 29 mid rt, P. 31 top rt, P. 34 top rt, P. 36 top rt, P. 37 top rt & mid rt, P. 40 top rt, P. 41 top lt, top rt, bot rt, bot strip, P. 43 top rt, P. 49 top, P. 56-57 photo spread, P. 56 bot rt, P. 57 top rt, mid rt, bot lt, P. 58 all photos, P. 59 mid rt, P. 64-65 spread, P. 68 all photos, P. 69 all photos, P. 70 all photos, P. 72 all photos, P. 73 mid, P. 75 bot rt, P. 92 top, P. 102-103 spread, P. 107 bot rt. P. 108 bot rt, P. 109 all photos, P. 110 all photos, P. 112 top rt, P. 114 top lt, P. 115 mid lt, P. 116 top lt P. 117 all photos, P. 118 all photos, P. 119 all photos, P. 121 mid photo, P. 120 mid rt, P. 133 all photos, P. 137 mid rt. P. 139 bot, P. 140 bot, P. 141 bot, P. 142 all photos, P. 147 top lt, P. 160 top lt. **ART BY TREVOR GORING:** P. 42 top storyboards, P. 54-55 top storyboards, P. 78 bot lt storyboard, P. 80 top rt storyboard, P. 81 two bot lt storyboard, P. 82-83 top lt/rt storyboard P. 84 three mid storyboards, P. 86 three bot rt storyboards, P. 92 bot two storyboards, P. 93 top & mid storyboards, P. 94 lt vertical storyboards, P. 96 mid storyboard, P. 109 bot storyboard, P. 110 mid storyboard, P. 111 bot storyboards, P. 113 storyboards, P. 114 top series storyboards P. 115 top story board, P. 117 lt vertical storyboards, P. 118 top storyboard, P. 120 top storyboard, P. 132 bot lt series storyboard, P. 133 top lt/ bot lt storyboard P. 138 top lt storyboard, **ART BY PHILIP KELLER:** P. 68 top/ bot storyboards, P. 69 top, bot/bot rt storyboards P. 70 top rt, bot lt storyboards, P. 72 top storyboard, P. 73 bot storyboard, P. 74-75 centerfold storyboard, P. 97-97 centerfold storyboard, P. 106-107 centerfold storyboard, P. 108 top, third from top storyboard, P. 109 top storyboard, P. 110 top/bot storyboard, P. 111 top storyboard, P. 112 storyboards, P. 114 bot storyboards, P. 115 mid storyboard, P. 118 mid lt, bot rt storyboard, P. 119 storyboards, P. 121 mid. lt, P. 126 storyboards, P. 127 storyboards, P. 128-131 storyboards, P. 132 bot lt storyboard, P. 133 mid lt storyboard, P. 135 storyboards, P. 138 top lt storyboard, P. 140 top two series storyboards, P. 142 storyboards. **ART BY DEANA NEWCOMB:** P. 21 top rt, P. 22, bot rt, P. 23 top lt, bot lt, P. 25 mid rt, P. 27 lower mid rt, P. 28 top rt, P. 31 mid rt, P. 35 top rt, P. 36 mid rt, P. 39 bot photos, P. 42 all photos, 43 mid rt, center, mid rt, center, mid, P. 46 all photos, P. 47 top rt, bot lt, bot rt, P. 48 all photos, P. 49 bot, P. 50 bot lt, P. 52 all photos, P. 53 all photos, P. 54 all photos, P. 55 all photos, P. 61 top rt, middle, P. 62 bot rt, P. 76-77 spread, P. 79 bot rt, P. 81 bot rt, P. 82 all photos, P. 83 bot, P. 85 bot lt, bot rt, P. 86 top rt, mid lt, bot lt, P. 87 all photos, P. 88-89 spread, P. 94 bot rt, P. 96 all photos, P. 98 bot lt, P. 99 all photos, P. 154 all photos, P. 155 all photos, P. 157 bot, bot rt, mid lt, bot mid lt, bot mid rt, P. 161 P. 160 mid lt & top lt, top rt, mid lt, center, mid rt, bot mid lt, bot rt, bot lt, P. 162 top lt, middle, P. 163 top middle rt., **ART © IRENE HARDWICKE OLIVIERI:** P. xii-3 paintings. **ART BY ERIN SCHNEIDER:** P. 3 top lt, bot rt photo.